I0624494

Inspiring Reviews for

INSPIRED

In "Inspired," Mutinta Nkombo-Kayumba crafts a rich and evocative memoir that brings to life the complexities of Zambian culture, family life, and personal ambition. Her storytelling blends humour, introspection, and a vivid sense of place, creating an engaging and earnest narrative. It reveals the changing economic landscapes of her family's journey, her own evolving identity, and an unwavering determination to succeed.

Mutinta's voice remains distinct and authentic throughout, drawing readers into her world with warmth and vulnerability. Her story is filled with ambition, love, and perseverance as she navigates her journey from a hotel receptionist to Miss Zambia Airways, ultimately becoming a wife and mother. Her life unfolds against the backdrop of a rapidly evolving Zambia, where personal dreams often collide with cultural expectations.

As she shares her family's journey, Mutinta also reveals the profound lessons learned from her mother. Her mother's strict yet loving upbringing instilled in her the values of resilience and adaptability that became crucial when facing adversity. Despite being judged harshly by others for leaving her marriage, Mutinta learned to prioritize self-love and preserve her sanity. The memoir shines brightest when conveying her relentless pursuit of education and health, even amidst the complexities of marriage and family life.

With poignant reflections, Mutinta delves into her own triumphs and trials, offering readers rare insights into her relentless pursuit of a better life.

Her journey, from balancing motherhood and business to prioritizing education and health despite personal challenges, remains relatable and inspirational. The resilience and adaptability she learned from her mother helped her overcome adversity and embrace change; making her story a testament to the transformative power of self-love and perseverance.

The book provides a candid glimpse into the author's unflinching honesty as she confronts the complexities of her journey. She encourages readers to navigate life's uncertainties with courage and grace by sharing her triumphs and struggles, offering a glimpse into the intricacies of Zambian society and the challenges of working motherhood.

Ultimately, Inspired is a compelling memoir that intricately weaves personal, familial, and societal narratives. Mutinta Nkombo-Kayumba's earnest writing transports readers into her world, highlighting the transformative power of embracing change and prioritizing self-love. The book is a celebration of resilience and the power of perseverance, making it a must-read for anyone interested in African memoirs, women's stories, and tales of overcoming challenges.

**"Professor Musonda Kapatamoyo,
Southern Illinois University Edwardsville"**

"Inspired" is one of the most remarkable books I have read in recent times. Mutinta's story not only draws one closer to her formidable personality, but also evokes strong emotions that many women can relate to. Her story is told with such great flare, authority, and courage. The revelations set us up well to discuss openly the challenges that women in Zambia and other parts of the world are faced with, the contemplation of whether to stay in a toxic relationship for the sake of societal "respect," or to leave and earn rebuke, rejection, and ridicule. "Inspired" leaves one with a bitter-sweet taste, as well as a sense of victory in Mutinta's courage and determination to overcome and rise above the water.

It is a brilliantly written publication worthy of international acclaim. We are proud of you, Mutinta. Well done.

Maureen Nkandu
Journalist, Author, Communications, and International Affairs Expert.

It's not common for a woman to talk (let alone write) about her life story, especially if it's 'marred' with challenges. To do so means you are going against the traditional norms in our predominantly patriarchal society, that teach us to keep silent and confine everything within the four walls. In her story, Mutinta exhibits a spirit of determination and resilience throughout her life. This especially is shown in her quest to improve her grade 12 certificate, an inspiration she got from her mother when the latter graduated at 72 years old. Mutinta realized that having a grounding in formal education was necessary, not for just getting a job, but in the running of businesses, which she's always been passionate about. This book is a must-read, because it is a lived account of Mutinta's life, a story that can inspire someone else who might have been, or is going through a similar situation. Ultimately, Mutinta demonstrates the importance of believing in oneself and focusing on what we love doing.

Mary Silavwe Mulenga
Author and Gender Activist - Zambia

It gives me great pleasure to recommend Mutinta Nkombo-Kayumba's poignant memoir, which is an inspiring account of her life's journey, told with unflinching tenacity and insightful real-life story. Through her masterful writing, Mutinta skillfully honours her mother, who moulded her and weaves a tapestry of fortitude, resilience, and insight. The story takes readers on a front-row seat to Mutinta's remarkable journey, as it unfolds in a beautiful tango, between the past and the present. As she overcomes obstacles and achieves success, with an uncommon combination of poise and resolve, her life narrative serves as a tribute to bravery and forethought.

The writing of Mutinta Nkombo Kayumba is extremely engaging and thought-provoking, making a lasting impression on readers. The transformational power of courage and foresight is demonstrated by the stories of ordinary people, who are celebrated in this book. I wholeheartedly recommend this book to anyone seeking inspiration, wisdom, and a deeper understanding of the human experience.

Dr. Burton Mweemba
Dean – School of Business
ZCAS University

The book is a must-read for the young, middle-aged, and elderly. The young ladies will be inspired to learn that the sky is not the limit. You can achieve greatness and that dreams do come true. They will also learn that the ending of the book… '*and they lived happily ever after,*' is actually the beginning, not the end of the story. The middle-aged will relate to the author's childhood stories. They will be inspired to introspect and adapt to new challenges life brings them, as well as learn new hobbies and breathe. The elderly will gracefully smile at their own past experiences and exhale. Some will pick themselves up and dust one or two things. Others will perhaps go back to school, write a book, and learn to swim, or go on a holiday to the Bahamas. The book will inspire anyone who reads it to do more, and be more!

Shupi Kayela Mweene ~ Mentee

INSPIRED

"Lessons from My Mother"

MUTINTA NKOMBO - KAYUMBA

ISBN: 978-1-965190-77-7

Table of Contents

Dedication

This book is dedicated to my dearest mother, Beatrice Musombai Muyaba, the incredible woman who firmly believes in discipline as a means of shaping a child's character. She unleashed all her energy to make me who I am today. Her unwavering strength, intelligence, determination, and overall attitude towards life, have been and continue to be my guiding principles. She has taught me that giving up is synonymous with failure.

Acknowledgements

To my handsome father Bernard, the greatest unifier. The most loving man I have ever known. His immeasurable love came with deep compassion, often displayed through his power of touch. He taught me that even a little was still enough for everyone to share. (MHSRIP)

To my dear siblings, Stella, Odiyee and Maynard (posthumously), Pitcairn, Choobe, Benny, Gary, Nchimunya, Cholwe, Nachilala, Munachande and Pamela, my greatest support system. The seamless team we are is a true testimony of how our father loved us by closely knitting us together.

To my lovely children, Mwaji and Mashuta, thank you for believing in me and carrying my limbs around with grace and dignity.

To my gorgeous grandchildren, Matthew-Teo and Kyeya-Mae, thank you for bringing a unique kind of love into my life. Your presence reminds me to slow down, and cherish every precious moment.

To my vitamin friends, the loving family I've chosen, thank you for uniquely supplementing my daily personal growth requirements.

To my husband Sande, for the life shared and for being a good father to my children.

Thank you

To Mr. Kwesi Atta Sakyi (posthumously), my lecturer at the Zambia Centre for Accountancy Studies, who supervised my Research Proposal during my MBA studies. At the beginning of the course, he asked each one of us to write on what inspired us to pursue the MBA program. He awakened my flare for writing and encouraged me to write more.

To my cousin Loyce and her husband Edwin Chanda, as well as my cousin Panic Malawo Chilufya, for their support. They provided a nurturing environment for me when I first left my parents' home, to start my first job in Lusaka. The collectivist nature of the Zambian society allowed for the extended family system to thrive, and they embraced me as their own. I will forever be thankful for their care and guidance.

To my cousin Panic, once again, my sister, Nchimunya Nkombo, my good friend, Josephine C.M. Faal, and my daughter, Mwaji Kayumba Mbalazi, for reviewing and editing the manuscript. Special thanks go to my sales assistant, Hazel Mkwanya, who has been tirelessly at my beck and calling for technical support.

To the editing team at Amazon Publishing Agency, thank you for the expertise and patience you exhibited throughout the development of the manuscript. I am thrilled to have reached this milestone.

Finally, I am filled with gratitude to God for his gracious hand of guidance, in transforming this visionary idea into a tangible reality.

About the Author

Mutinta Nkombo Kayumba, born in 1968, comes from a family of school teachers. She is a wife, mother of two, and a grandmother to two grandchildren. Her education began at Mulwani Primary School in Livingstone, followed by Mazabuka Girls Secondary School in the Southern Province of Zambia.

After completing high school, Mutinta started her career as a receptionist at Fairmount Hotel in Livingstone. She later transitioned to Eagle Travel and Tours, a service company, where she worked as a Tour Guide. Seeking new opportunities, she relocated to Lusaka and joined the Zambia National Provident Fund as an Accounts Clerk.

Mutinta's aspiration to become an air hostess became a reality when she responded to a job advertisement by Zambia Airways in the newspapers, and she successfully secured a position as a cabin attendant, and later became the face of the national airline.

Following the liquidation of Zambia Airways in 1994, Mutinta shifted her focus to her business, which gradually became her primary occupation. Alongside managing her business, she pursued further education at the Chartered Institute of Marketing in the United Kingdom (UK), where she obtained a Chartered Post Graduate Diploma in Marketing. Motivated to enhance her knowledge, she then enrolled at the University of Greenwich in the UK, where she earned her Master of Business Administration degree with a specialization in International Business.

Currently, Mutinta continues to run her business successfully, which has grown organically due to her resilience and financial discipline.

Preface

As I reflect on my childhood, one of the things I remember often doing, was answering the question, "What do you want to be when you grow up?" with a consistent response being: an air-hostess. This aspiration stemmed from the fascination I developed during our family trips to Livingstone airport, where we would watch planes take off and land.

Additionally, a movie I watched as a child showcased the air hostesses' impeccable uniforms, coordinated movements, flawless makeup, and stylish hairstyles, which left a lasting impression on me. The idea of providing service at high altitude seemed glamorous and appealing.

Despite this childhood dream, I ultimately applied to study Education at the University of Zambia, influenced by my parents, who were both school teachers. However, I questioned whether I possessed the necessary patience and resilience to excel in teaching. Failing to gain admission into university felt like a family tragedy, but deep down, I felt a sense of consolation because teaching was not my true calling.

While contemplating my next move, I decided to apply for a receptionist position at the New Fairmount Hotel, (NFH) in Livingstone. Although my father disapproved of the high level of customer interaction involved in the job, he reluctantly allowed me to pursue it, recognizing my need for personal growth and fulfilment. Working at NFH not only provided me with a sense of independence and responsibility, but also allowed me to earn my own money to purchase clothing, makeup, perfumes, and even groceries for my family.

Through my work, I had the opportunity to interact with people from diverse backgrounds, as NFH was often the preferred choice for guests who could not secure accommodation, at the prestigious Hotel Intercontinental, Mosi-O-Tunya, near Victoria Falls.

One day, while on duty, a Sunday Times reporter captured my image, and featured it in the Sunday Girl column. The article did not contain a specific story but simply mentioned that I worked as a receptionist at NFH in Livingstone.

Following the publication, the switchboard buzzed endlessly, and while fidgeting to answer and pondering how to handle numerous callers who were looking for one Mutinta, I heard my father's voice on the other end in a way I had never heard it before. "Mutinta, you are not for Sunday Girl," he went on and on. I kept still, and then I heard him say, "Are you there?" I managed to say yes, Father." We will continue this conversation at home," and with that, he hung up. I thanked God that he had no idea that the switchboard was buzzing incessantly. Luckily for me, I was quickly taken out of NFH as I got a job with Eagle Travel and Tours. That brought an end to the calls.

The pay at Eagle Travel was slightly better, and I did not have to do shift work, though the nature of work was pretty much the same, with a high customer interface. My father was still not satisfied with this job, so he made me apply to Chainama College of Health Sciences in Lusaka to train as a Medical Officer, something that had never crossed my mind. Sadly, for him I failed to get in; I was not cut for the medical profession either; moreover, my science results were very weak. I then applied to the Zambia National Provident Fund, and was given a job as an Accounts Clerk, before I landed my dream job as an air hostess, at Zambia Airways (QZ).

I not only became an air hostess, but I also became Miss Zambia Airways, and subsequently, the face of the national airline. This resulted in me joining the marketing team, which was promoting Zambia Airways globally. The Miss Zambia Airways crown was achieved by going through a rigorous cabin service contest that focused on safety and service proficiency. Indeed, my life changed instantly one evening when Stanley Makulu, the Master of Ceremonies of the contest, announced that I had scooped the Miss Zambia Airways title for the year 1990.

Gripped with the most profound anxiety, I emerged from the holding room where the other contestants and I were trying to manage our anxieties with some alcoholic beverages. I beat eleven other contestants to be crowned Miss Zambia Airways. The contest was graced by the then Minister of Transport and Communications, Brigadier General Enos Haimbe. The reigning Miss Zambia Airways for the year 1989, my dear friend Josephine Chilufya Mukuka, handed over the trophy to me amid cheers of my name. The prize included fully-paid up local tours to Livingstone and Kasaba Bay, K15,000,000.00 cash (fifteen million Kwacha un-rebased) a trip for two to the Bahamas Islands, plus $2,000.00 (two thousand United States dollars) spending money.

As a twenty-two-year-old, I took the trip up to New York with two men: my brother, Gary, and my boyfriend, Sande, who later became my husband. For many reasons, we decided to terminate the trip to the Bahamas in New York. The foregone trip to the Bahamas Islands propelled my entrepreneurial journey into the business person I am today. In lieu of the trip to the Bahamas, we opted to buy boxes and boxes of TDK cassettes, which we managed to resell when we got back home.

During my short working life at NFH, my path crossed with that of one Colonel in the Zambia Air Force (ZAF), Sande, who later became my husband and father to my lovely children, Mwaji and Mashuta.

I married Sande in 1991 at a colourful ceremony that was characterized by military wedding etiquette. Sande rose through the ranks and was appointed Commander of the Zambia Air Force early in our marriage.

Upon getting married, my life went through a drastic change. I moved from the Young Women's Christian Association (YWCA) hostel, where I used to live, to a house opposite the Zambian President's residency (State House). While still getting used to the fame that accompanied my new title of Miss Zambia Airways, I gravitated towards more exposure as an Air Force Commander's wife. I attended several state functions and got to mix closely with eminent people in society.

The first life my children were exposed to was that of being Air Force Commander's children, although they were too young to appreciate or make sense of it. We were always driven around by uniformed personnel, and we had sentries guarding us around the clock. At the gate, my kith and kin had to answer the question "Is Mrs Kayumba expecting you?" every time they came to see me. But frustratingly, my new life as the Commander's wife was low on dos, and high on don'ts. It was totally different from the high-flying world of Zambia Airways, to which I had become accustomed.

Apart from the school life my children had at Musikili Primary School in Southern Zambia, this was the only other life they had ever known, having military protection twenty-four-seven.

Following my husband's retirement, I realized that they got so wired to that lifestyle; they were too scared to even cross the road.

The change in our circumstances finally gave me time to concentrate on my business. Zambia Airways oriented me to a practice of trading as a side hustle. Every time I travelled, I would buy all sorts of merchandise, which I would resell to the Indian business community in Kamwala and the Central Business District (CBD). With Zambia Airways gone, and my husband's job in our past, I knew that I had to take up the baton to ensure we maintained the same, if not a better lifestyle. What began as a side hustle eventually became my main hustle.

In my entrepreneurial journey, I scored many firsts. In 1998, Sande and I partnered to open a boutique called Genuine Collections, a clothing store in Lusaka's Central Business District, which stocks the finest apparel for both ladies and gentlemen.

In 2001, I was among the pioneers in the guest house business, when I founded the Comfort Lodge. It did not take long before I saw a business opportunity for market growth. This was driven by growing concerns about too much traffic in the CBD of Lusaka, where Genuine Collections is still situated.

In 2012, I scored a first, when I opened the first-ever residential boutique at Comfort Lodge, which was in Jesmondine, a suburb near the University of Zambia. This concept was initially criticized by many, but just as I had envisaged, it flourished, and then I saw the competition imitate it. The residential boutique concept took away a lot of pressure and was embraced by most of my customers. It also gave me a competitive advantage because I was trading from my own space; I had the flexibility of keeping this outlet open until late, because it was situated in a safe neighbourhood.

In 2017, I decided to tap into another market, the Woodlands Suburb. I walked into the office of Mr. Eric Shultz, the American Ambassador to the Republic of Zambia, and requested him to officially open my signature outlet. He accepted. At a colourful launch characterized with pomp and splendour, he insisted that we cut the ribbon together, and graciously, we did; Genuine Outfitters was born.

Before then, I undertook to improve my grade twelve certificate, which had weak grades in some subjects. After that, I enrolled in a Marketing course with the Chartered Institute of Marketing (CIM) in the United Kingdom. I was multi-tasking roles: motherhood, wife, businesswoman, and patron of the ZAF women's club known as the Air-Power ladies club. I found I had too much on my plate and soon abandoned my Marketing course. I then went on to enrol at Cavendish University to pursue a Bachelor of Business Administration degree, which I also abandoned.

My mother, Beatrice Muyaba, is my greatest inspiration. At the age of 72, she defied age and made newspaper headlines when she graduated with a Bachelor's degree in Adult Education from the Zambia Open University. When this happened, I felt challenged, but inspired and told myself that I had no excuse for dropping out of pursuing further studies. My mother encouraged me to go back to school, and repeatedly said to me that education is the best investment for the future, and that giving up is synonymous with failure.

A desperate call to CIM confirmed that I was still a registered studying member with only one course to go in order to attain a full certificate. The voice on the other side of the phone, however, warned that if I did not resume my studies that same year, I would lose all my credits. I made a witting decision to get back into class.

I quickly attained my Certificate and proceeded to my Diploma course, and thereafter, the Chartered Post Graduate Diploma. This was probably the most humbling time of my life, to find myself in class learning with kids of my children's age.

After attaining the Post-Graduate Diploma in Marketing, I received an invitation to attend the graduation ceremony in 2013, at Church House, Westminster, England. I graduated alongside several other like-minded people from Zambia. While I was still excited about conquering Marketing, I decided to pursue a Master of Business Administration degree in International Business, at the University of Greenwich, UK.

Suddenly, I realized that I had put myself under a new kind of pressure; I was studying at the same time with my children, Mwaji and Mashuta, who were also in university. I was under more pressure than them, as I could not imagine failing, while they passed. The experience reminded me of how I used to tell them that if they failed, they were on their own. Undoubtedly, the three of us were under pressure. I graduated with distinction in 2016. My children said that I left them under immense pressure, but they also managed to graduate soon after me.

Shortly after school, Mwaji decided to grow our family. She got married to her best friend, Musonda Mbalazi. They gave me the most gorgeous grandchildren, Matthew-Teo, 4, and Kyeya-Mae, 2.

I started thinking about writing my memoirs on my birthday on 6th February of 2019, while in Livingstone, where I was taking care of my dear mother, who was diagnosed with dementia. Sadly, the Covid-19 pandemic crept into our country like a thief in the night.

I put the idea aside because my businesses, 'like many others,' were threatened; there were no customers, as "quarantine" was the buzzword.

I made alternative arrangements for my mother's care, to enable me to rush back to Lusaka, to give direction to my businesses. It was challenging both socially and economically. The economic strain brought about by the pandemic forced me to drastically scale down. Comfort Lodge had to close. Furthermore, travel to most countries was restricted, I had to close the boutique at Comfort Lodge too.

Covid-19 was a global pandemic, and for a long time, there was no ray of hope of a vaccine in sight. For the first time, the adage "United we stand and divided we fall" could no longer hold. "United we fall and divided we stand" became more fashionable. Self-isolation became the world order, and everyone was cocooned in their personal spaces.

During that period, I left my matrimonial home, because my marriage was severely challenged. It was not the easiest of things to move away from a life I had known for twenty-eight years.

As part of my therapy, I did cycling, walking, golf, swimming, and gardening, all in search of my endorphins. Sauna and massage completed the whole wellness regimen. I often took the longest drives, sometimes to Nowhere-ville, just to fill the void. Inevitably, I enrolled in counselling, midway through, I convinced myself that I could fill the void by writing my memoirs.

Chapter 1
A Life Unveiled

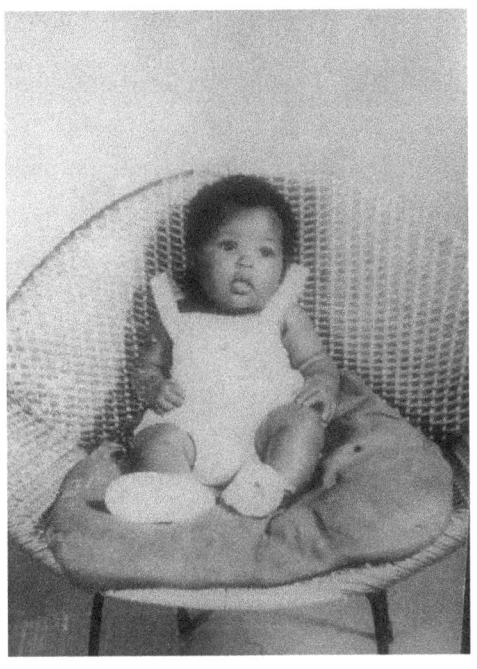

Mutinta at the age of six months

My mother sat on the veranda, focusing on her grandchildren, who were cooling off in the swimming pool. We were at my home in Woodlands. Three overgrown Bonsai trees are in competition with the veranda pillars. Images of white ducks swimming in turquoise waters are hanging on the wall opposite each other. A fully stocked bar is snuggled in the right corner, a television set is hanging above the bar unit, the floral finish covering the bamboo chairs, completes my veranda setting.

It was my 53rd birthday. I started my day with a sauna bath and then set off to celebrate my birthday with the saints at Kabwata Orphanage. Accompanied by my two children, Mwaji and Mashuta, we took an assortment of foodstuffs for the children there. After the presentation, the children sang Happy Birthday to me, we ate cake with them, after which my children took me out for lunch at D'lila Restaurant.

Back home, my mother Beatrice was still seated on what seemed to be her permanent seat. My mother is of medium height, medium dark in complexion, an intelligent and self-actualized woman with a curvy frame. Clad in bright yellow Ankara design, her silence spoke to a great extent that I had taken longer than she expected. I had made an appointment to interview her about my childhood, and exactly how I came to be. She vividly recalled that when she was expecting me, there was speculation from a traditional midwife who was her friend, that she was carrying twins, because that pregnancy was much bigger compared to her earlier two.

Before me, she had two boys, Benny and Gary. The same midwife helped her deliver the boys, so it was easy to believe her. It was because of this, that she and my father decided that she be taken to Chikankata Hospital for a professional opinion and subsequent delivery. Chikankaka Hospital was one of the best hospitals in southern Zambia then, so it was a safe option too.

My mother recalled that at that time, there was a serious fuel shortage, but my father used his networks and managed to secure some fuel in order to drive her to the hospital. Through a mere examination of seeing, touching, and feeling, the staff at the hospital joined in the speculation that my mother was carrying twins. She still had two weeks to her delivery due date; hence, my father who was in formal employment, had no choice but to leave her under the care of the hospital staff. After two weeks, she delivered. I made a solo entry into the world, making the twin story a classic miss.

She narrated that she delivered the most beautiful baby girl, much to the marvel of the hospital staff, and in her own words, she said she could just see her husband in her baby. She also narrated how I was nearly swapped with another baby.

The nurse accidentally passed on the wrong baby to her for feeding. She had watched the nurse getting confused in the handing out of babies for feeding, so she refused to take that baby, and asked the nurse to double-check with the name tags before handing out babies.

I had been given to the wrong mother, who seemed okay with just being given a baby to breastfeed without checking the baby's details. My mother has told this story severally to all my siblings, on how she kept vigil for fear of losing me. When they want to get at me, they jokingly tease that I may have really been swapped. Luckily, I turned out to be a replica of my father, and I am firmly reassured by that.

This was the era of letters and telegrams, and my mother was unable to inform my father that she had delivered. Even if she wrote a letter, she had no way of posting it, as she was still recovering. So, with me in her arms and bags on her back, she boarded a bus from Chikankata Hospital to Mazabuka town. She arrived at her friend Sarah's place, where she asked Sarah and her husband Moses Hamusunse to drive her to her home in Monze rural. When we arrived home, my father Bernard was just parking his Datsun 1200 van, coming from the post office where he had gone to post a letter, to find out how my mother was doing. They were very happy to be blessed with a girl.

Together, they agreed to name me Mutinta, meaning 'change', after having had two boys. My parents were both school teachers, teaching at a school called Chungu, where we lived in a teacher's compound. My mother narrated that I started my school as an informal scholar at the age of five.

My mother was a Grade 1 teacher at the same school. She narrated that each time she left for school, I gave her only a few minutes to get busy, and settle into her class. In a swift style, I would quietly sneak into her class and sit at the back. The teacher-pupil ratio was high, so it would take a long time for her to notice that I was in class.

My mother Beatrice and father Bernard in their early days.

However, each time she saw me at the back of her class, she made it a point to take me back home at break time because she thought I was too young to start school. I was never deterred. I would wait for her to settle in after break time, before I could sneak back in again. When she got tired of chasing me, she let me carry on. In her mind, I was just passing time quietly in her class. At the end of the year, when she was assessing her students, she decided to give me a test as well. I performed much better than most of the registered students, much to her amazement. She then saw it prudent for me to proceed to Grade 2.

When I was six years old, my parents moved to Livingstone, where I was typically raised. The first house we lived in was within the Livingstone Trades Training Institute compound for lecturers. It was a basic house with conveniences placed outside. My parents' home was always full of relatives. We lived with cousins, aunties, and uncles, but we were all raised as one. Sleeping was always a challenge; sometimes, we slept on beds, and sometimes on the floor, and when there were visitors, it was not strange to find one sleeping in the living room.

I was born in a family of thirteen, four boys and nine girls. Growing up, we found ourselves in clusters, guided by our ages. In my cluster were Choobe, Ben, Gary, and myself. We had no television set at home, so the four of us closely bonded because we ultimately depended on each other for entertainment.

Our meals were mostly vegetarian, not by choice, but because that was what my parents could afford. The four of us had a pact that at meal times and during rare times when we had some non-vegetarian food, one of us would be the one to share equal portions of the available relish. Choobe was assigned to share out beef, Ben shared out chicken, Gary shared out fish, and I had to share out eggs.

After that, we picked our portions in order of seniority. Eggs were only eaten once in a very blue moon, so that meant that I rarely had the opportunity to share, and even when I was accorded the chance to share, I was always the last one to pick my share as I was the youngest in my cluster. I could always tell just by looking at the portions which one was mine, because it was always the smallest.

Christmas time brought special memories because once in a year, we were assured of getting new clothes. We had special meals such as rice with chicken and cake for dessert. We also got to drink the coveted Coca-Cola and Fanta. At times, my brother Ben would entice me to slip a small pebble in my Coca-Cola bottle, so that I could get more of it. That created some chemical reaction that would make it overflow, and by the time I realized it, all the drink was gone. What followed was a waterfall on my face, and that was my Christmas treat down the drain. A desperate explanation to my mother sometimes managed to secure me another one.

Our everyday drink was a delicious drink made from maize grits, which when mixed with Munkoyo roots, and sometimes fermented sweet potato peels, soaked in water, produced a drink called *Chibwantu*. This drink has clearly stood the test of time, as it has now found itself on the shelves of Zambian supermarkets.

My parents were trying to adjust to a new lifestyle, having come out of Monze rural into Livingstone. My father had a friend called Trywell Himoonga who, together with his family, welcomed and helped us to settle in the urban setting. Mr Trywell Himoonga was the Headmaster for Mulwani Primary School, which was right next to the Livingstone Trades Training Institute, where we lived.

My parents and the Himoongas used to socialize together a lot. Each time my parents went to visit them, we tagged along to just watch television or play a game of fire with their children.

Oftentimes, we would go to the Himoongas on our own, which simply meant that we went without getting permission. On this one fateful day, Gary and I secretly followed our father to the Himoongas, thinking he would be there until 21.00 hours as per usual.

We played a game called Touch, where two teams faced off on a rectangular field, aiming to touch a ball into the opposing team's goal area. Ideally, the game is played with an oval-shaped ball, similar to a rugby ball, but since we couldn't afford one, we created our own makeshift. After a fired game of touch, we realized that it was several minutes past 20:00 hours. A check at the Himoongas' living room just revealed darkness. My father had left us because he had no idea that we had secretly followed him.

It was dark, and the darkness was monstrous. Hand in hand, Gary and I navigated through the teachers' compound in a desperate attempt to get to the institute. Apart from the uncertainty of the darkness, we knew that we were in trouble at home and mostly with my mother. While walking home, we suddenly saw two figures walking towards us. Could they be thieves? We asked each other. Simultaneously, Gary and I reduced our speed, and retreated with backward steps as if we were under military orders. Gripped with so much fear, we continued going forward, albeit much slower.

As the figures got closer, the gait resembled that of my mother, and the other of her sister, Aunt Agnes. And when it became evident that they were the ones, we both knew that we were about to take a trip to hell, because my mother seldom spared the rod. She got Gary by his arm, Aunt Agnes grabbed mine, and we were marched home. We knew that was not the end of the ordeal, so we started crying ahead of time, with the hope that my mother would feel sorry for us.

Alas, we got home where she had mulberry tree whips always ready. She took turns at Gary and I, not only because we had sneaked out, but largely because we also got ourselves so dirty after the game of Touch. Inevitably, we had to bath again.

The aftermath of that walloping was a bath, in the bathroom outside of the house, in what felt like ice-cold water. I remember crying through the bathing session, and thereafter crying myself to sleep.

My late father was fair-skinned, tall, lean, handsome, and by all means, a great networker. He used this advantage for his own good. It didn't take long before he secured a house in the Mulwani School compound, which was slightly bigger, better, electrified, and had a water closet inside. We continued trying to adapt to the urban settings, some of which were frankly quite shocking. Our parents could neither afford a television nor a radio set yet, so the trips to our neighbors continued, except now they were with full consent from them.

There was a positive to all this. When we didn't go to watch television with the neighbours, we listened to our parents' wise counsel. We took turns to tell and listen to each other's stories, something we have carried to our adult age. As a result, we grew up closely-knit, and the display of our shared values is envied by many.

My father believed in strong family ties. He always wanted us to stay close to his mother. When the cluster grew a bit older, it was his style to bundle us in his Datsun 1200 open van, every single holiday and drive us to the village at Munenga, in Magoye, where my grandmother Choobe Nkombo lived with her sister Chooka Kambole. The two lived in a big, one-roomed, rotunda-shaped thatched house where each one had a single bed. Our bed was somewhere in the middle, on the floor. The two sisters were old and widowed, but one could see through their wrinkles that beauty once lived there. Life in the village was not new to us, because we had just come out of Monze rural, where life was pretty much the same.

The order of the day was to wake up, go and fetch water, make a fire, clean the house, and go to the maize field.

One person always remained at home to prepare the meals while the rest of us went to the fields. Somehow, everyone preferred to stay at home to do the house chores rather than go to the fields. Most times, breakfast consisted of sweet potatoes and black tea made out of burnt sugar. A few times, when someone went to town, we would have real tea with bread. *Chibwantu* was sometimes brought to the fields, and sometimes there was none.

The whole routine was so monotonous, laborious, and long that we would lose count of the days. We looked forward to the evenings when we would all be bathed and would sit around the fire to listen to stories from our two grannies who got on like a house on fire. At the weekend, they would dress up in their long-flared skirts, jackets, and hats. They would then carry their own homemade brew to their local pub, to chill out with their friends. Later in the night, we would hear them either singing or bickering as they walked back home; we were too young and innocent to know that it was the same brew that they carried that got them drunk.

There was absolutely no other form of communication then, apart from letters and telegrams. Moreover, the post office was far from the village. The only sign that the holiday was coming to an end was the cranking sound of my father's Datsun 1200, and the dust that followed it when he came to pick us up. The sight of it was always received with immense joy as it was an assurance that we had two days to go back to town.

Chapter 2
Growing Up

Mutinta at the age of 16.

Life was so humbling as we saw our parents struggle to feed, clothe, and educate us all. Luckily, they could afford to get each one of us a pair of shoes which we wore until we outgrew them. The shoes had to work for church, school and any other occasion. In their haggard state, they were then handed down to our younger siblings. In order to make ends meet, my mother would make scones, fry groundnuts, and rear chickens to sell in order to raise some extra money.

We attended school from 07:30 hours in the morning up to 12:30 hours, and then in the afternoon, we became salespeople, taking turns selling my mother's merchandize at Dambwa market in Livingstone. We used to sell chickens, groundnuts, or scones. At other times, we sold oranges and vitumbuwas (doughnuts). Our tasks were very clear: to sell it all, as we were encouraged not to return home with unsold merchandise. At times, it was hard to find buyers, but we soldiered on, knowing that having all the merchandise sold was raising our standard of living.

My father was later posted to head Namatama Primary School in Livingstone. Namatama was quite far from Mulwani School, making it difficult for him to commute every day. He was then given a house in the Namatama School teacher's compound, because it also did not augur well for him to be the headmaster at Namatama

School while living in the Mulwani School compound. We had no choice but to move. Namatama was a much smaller school with fewer streams. The house was also smaller than where we were coming from, but we again had to adapt. Inevitably, all of us had to change schools from Mulwani to Namatama School. My mother's business was greatly affected because we had moved into a new area, so she needed to identify new markets for her merchandise. During this time, we got ourselves some time off from selling.

Namatama School brought us close to Henry Nkolola, my father's cousin, with his wife Evelyn, who lived in Nottie Broad. Henry, like my father, was a full-bodied, handsome man, who worked at the Education office. Henry married a South African lady called Evelyn. Evelyn was a short, fair, and very soft-spoken lady. We were introduced to their children, who we quickly got attached to. I particularly got close to Catherine Nkolola, who was one year older than me. Catherine is one assertive beauty, medium in height with an espresso complexion. Catherine and I enjoyed chatting with one another, and to date, we still have our talking sessions. We basically did a lot of things together, which made our friendship grow. Unfortunately for us, we did not stay very long at the Namatama School compound.

My father managed to rent a council house through his strong networking skills. At that time, James Mapala, one of his good friends, was Livingstone Council Town Clerk. James made it happen for his friend, and he used his discretion to allocate a house to my father, which he rented from the council. It meant that Catherine and I were a good distance away from each other. This, however, did not stop us. Every weekend, we would plan to meet, so we took turns walking the almost one-and-a-half-kilometre distance between our homes in order to see one another.

When we didn't walk to each other's home, we met at the Cool and Sound Centre for a teen time gig. As we grew older and evolved, we inevitably made different choices, causing out paths to diverge, and fork in separate directions.

In a remarkable twist of fate, Catherine and I experienced a unique convergence of paths. We both relocated to Lusaka, where I became a flight attendant, and she joined the military as a lady officer. In a fascinating turn of events, my husband was appointed Air Force Commander, and Catherine, then a captain, served as his secretary. Despite our differing roles, she graciously addressed me as "Madam," though it felt somewhat awkward. Interestingly, Catherine married David Muma, a fellow Livingstone native, and Air Force officer, who later rose through the ranks to attain the highest command, in the Air Force. In a beautiful stroke of fate, Catherine and I, found ourselves on equal footing once again.

My stay in Livingstone also got me close to friends like Sandra Muma, who I met through a wedding line up, and Doreen Anakene Haangala, who I met through my childhood play dates, and later met again at Eagle Travel and Tours, where we both worked as Tour Guides. We have grown together and managed to reasonably rub our friendship onto our children.

22 Kombe Drive was not only bigger but also in a good residential area, by and large, a very good house. When the "New Deal" government of the late Zambian President Frederick Chiluba announced the sale of all council and government houses, my mother managed to purchase 22 Kombe Drive. I remember very well how hard it was then for my parents to furnish it. We now had a designated bedroom for boys and for girls, although there would easily be ten girls in one room during holidays.

At times when we had visitors, it was much easier for my parents to displace the boys to the worker's quarters, to pave way for the guests. The boys loved that arrangement because it earned them some freedom to go out to the disco.

For the first time, we had a house with running hot water, so bathing was such a pleasure. My parents managed to buy the first refrigerator, much to our delight. We could now drink cold water to quench the thirst of the torrid Livingstone weather. We clearly were mesmerized by the fact that in the deep freezer, water quickly turned into ice. That presented a business opportunity for us too. So, we started selling sweetened ice blocks. We used to put cream soda or strawberry cordials in small plastics and freeze them overnight to make ice blocks for sale the next day.

Up to the time we moved to Kombe Drive, we still did not have a television set. At Kombe Drive, the neighbourhood was strange to us. We needed to make friends very quickly in order to watch television from somewhere.

We befriended the children of the family next door, who seemed to have it all. Mr. Bwalya, our neighbour, was a locomotive driver working for Zambia Railways. We saw very little of him because he worked at night mostly. The few times we saw him, we exclaimed at how he looked so good in his uniform. His wife Martha, was a midwife at the Livingstone General Hospital, and she also did shift work.

The Bwalyas were very neighbourly, so permission was granted for us to watch television from their home. Their nature of work entailed that, most times they were not home, so their house became the perfect playground for us. We used to have wonderful times there playing fire, hopscotch, and a battery game called killer.

When playing fire, we divided ourselves into two teams, and tried to eliminate all the team players on the opposing team, by hitting them with a ball. The team that managed to eliminate all the players got to win. In hopscotch, we took turns hopping on one foot through a series of numbered squares, starting with the square where a marker was tossed. The player must hop to the square with the marker, pick it up, and continue to the next square. If they step on a line, miss a square, or lose balance, their turn ends. However, there were times when we found ourselves in conflict with the Bwalya children. It went without saying that during those times, there would be no games or television to watch.

It did not take long before my father was transferred from Namatama to Dambwa Primary School in the same capacity. Dambwa Primary was closer to home in comparison to Namatama. We were also transferred back to Mulwani Primary School, which was nearer to Kombe Drive. By this time, my father had bought a yellow Mazda car after selling his Datsun 1200 van, which had been giving him problems. We nicknamed the Mazda car, New Zealand lamb for some reason I cannot remember.

Clearly, there was an upgrade in our lives because sometimes we were taken to school by a saloon car, but oftentimes, it was fun to walk with friends. Even if walking was a fun activity, older kids often took advantage of us by bullying us. No one would dare bully me and get away with it. I had an army of older siblings.

One day, my friend Arlene Hamusunse (daughter to my mother's friend Sarah) and I were walking through the institute to school. We were tiny little girls. Arlene looked even smaller because she was shorter than me. A girl called Florence stopped us and started beating us up. The two of us were too timid to even hit back.

Choobe appeared from nowhere to rescue us. She beat up Florence until she bled. This obviously did not sit well with Florence's mother. She attempted to come and see our mother to register a complaint, but Choobe, being very fearless, made some whips from the mulberry tree, and challenged Florence's mother to dare get close to the house. Florence's mother chickened out.

There was a lot of yard space at Kombe Drive. Mother decided to start a poultry project, and it did not take very long before the capacity increased. In no time, we were back at Dambwa market, selling chickens. My mother's entrepreneurial mind also led her to Botswana, where she started cross-border trading to afford us a decent life. She used to buy groceries, watches, Puma blankets, and all sorts of merchandise for resale. This business had a good return on investment for her, so she continued going back and forth.

The first sign of prosperity in the cross-border business for my mother was her ability to buy a beautiful bedroom and dining suite. As time went by, our parents managed to acquire a television set. With the cross-border trading that my mother had embarked on, the chicken-rearing business was now behind us. In any case, our cluster was moving into boarding schools, and there were no other salespeople.

Chapter 3
High School

I wrote my Grade 7 examinations in 1979 and qualified to Mazabuka Girls Secondary School in 1980. The school was well known for its academic excellence in the Southern Province then. Grade seven results were always published way after the first term had started, which meant that I had to go to school on my own, because my cluster mates had already gone back to school at the beginning of the term.

The only mode of transport our parents could afford was the Zambia Railways train, which left Livingstone at midnight and arrived in Mazabuka the next day. Arlene and I both qualified to go to Grade 8 (Form 1 then). Our friendship was inspired by our parents, who were also good friends. My mother always told me how Arlene's mother, Sarah, mentored her and encouraged her to improve her education.

Arlene's sister, late Anne Hamusunse, a former Mazabuka Girl's student, was assigned by Arlene's parents to escort us to school. We boarded the Luangwa train at midnight, seen off by our parents. The apprehension on their faces was noticeable, and they unleashed numerous instructions on us. We were excited at the idea of being independent of them, but we dreaded the mocking that was prevalent in most schools then.

The three of us arrived in Mazabuka the next morning. Anne organized for me to be dropped off at my Uncle Franklin's home. Uncle Frank was a politician in the first Zambian republic. He was a Member of Parliament for Mazabuka Central and held many other portfolios in the government. His driver drove me to school, where I met up with Arlene later in the day.

We arrived to a warm welcome from my cousins, late Caroline Malawo, Jane Maulu, and Arlene's late sister, Annette Hamusunse. After doing all the formalities for us, Anne handed us over to the trio and returned to Livingstone the same day.

Arlene and I were fortunate to be allocated bed space in the same dormitory, to be sleeping next to each other on bunkers, on top of Caroline and Jane's beds. With the two sleeping below us, we knew that we would not be bullied by anyone.

I recall how hard it was for both of us to get to sleep the first night. It was a strange environment for us. I personally had never slept on a bunker bed. I was scared that I would roll over and drop to the floor. Despite the assurances we had received when we first arrived at the school, we were still scared, so we repeatedly called each other out, "Mutinta, have you slept?" Arlene would ask, and after a while, I would return the same question to her, "Arlene, have you slept?" Minute by minute and hour after hour, we continued checking on each other.

Somewhere in the darkness, we got tired of asking each other the same question. We each lay still in our beds, and then the only sound coming through was the squeaking of the roof, and finally, sleep claimed us.

High school brought us closer together despite our frequent childish fights. We would often find ourselves at odds, going for weeks without speaking, but when we finally reconciled, there was always plenty to talk about. After high school, our paths diverged due to the different choices we made, but our friendship remained strong. Although we don't get to see each other frequently, when we do reunite for lunch, it inevitably stretches into dinner, as we have so much to catch up on.

High school exposed me to a diverse array of individuals, from those hailing from affluent backgrounds to those in greater need than myself. I survived on basic supplies like bathing soap, washing powder, toothpaste, sugar, and bread. I relied on the provisions my parents could afford, though they seldom lasted until the term's end. The school diet primarily featured cabbage and beans, and when seeking variety, I resorted to a sugar and water solution known as "zigolo," complemented by bread. In times of scarcity, the generosity of my cousins, Jane and Aze sustained me.

I found myself in a team of affluent girls. We formed a group calling ourselves the Six Million Dollar Ladies. I do not even know how this happened because they were all older than me. The group members were Monica Phiri, Nyambe Mutemwa, Margaret Simbotwe, Sylvia Chanda, my cousin Aze Malawo and myself.

Our discussions centred on television shows and life in Lusaka, topics that often left me on the periphery, due to my different life experiences. Parent Teachers' Day highlighted the economic disparities among students, as some were laden with goodies from their parents while others, like me, sat with the awareness that our parents could not afford such luxuries.

Despite these challenges, I held firm to the belief that academic performance would shape my future. As an average student, weak in sciences but inclined toward the arts, I discovered my creative side. The Grade 12 examinations in 1984 brought an unexpected twist, a surprising 7 in my English language examination, a setback that marred my certificate and barred entry to the University of Zambia. This inexplicable failure haunted me, leaving a trail of sadness and amplifying the disappointment of my parents, who saw it not just as my failure but theirs as well, considering their roles as school teachers.

Chapter 4
Working Life

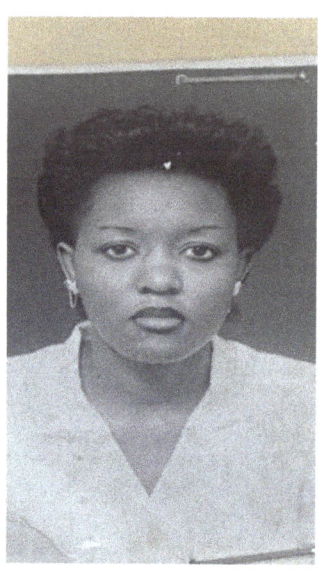

Mutinta ready to go for an interview as air-hostess at Zambia Airways-1988.

As I contemplated my next move, fortune smiled upon me, granting me a job as a receptionist at the New Fairmount Hotel, in Livingstone. My parents made it clear that this was a temporal measure; they expected me to return to school at the right time while aiming to enhance my certificate for university admission. My tenure at NFH brought a sense of satisfaction, as I earned a salary that could meet my immediate needs.

However, the drawback was the shift work, occasionally making me arrive home after midnight due to transportation constraints. This schedule did not sit well with my parents, especially my over-protective father.

As the first point of contact for hotel customers, I became well-known in my role. However, this visibility stirred concerns from my parents, leading my father to orchestrate an attempt to redirect my career path. He arranged for me to attend Chainama College of Health Sciences in Lusaka, to train as a Medical Officer. Despite the misalignment with my passion and the weakness in my sciences, I complied with the aptitude tests out of respect for my father. Predictably, I failed the tests, compelling me to continue working at the hotel.

I believed that I had a good relationship with my general manager, Jane, much to my chagrin. Surprisingly, one day, she summoned me to her office and abruptly terminated my employment, without providing any reason. This action occurred beyond my probation period, leaving me puzzled and defenceless. Timid and uninformed about labour dispute resolutions, I accepted my fate. When I informed my front office manager, Rose, of the dismissal, she encouraged me to wait and not go home.

In recognition of my capabilities, Rose took it upon herself to confront Jane and the hotel's owners, the Naidoo family. Jane remained unconvinced, but the Naidoos overturned her decision, and I was reinstated the next morning. Grateful for Rose's intervention, I returned to work but with a heightened awareness of my strained relationship with Jane. Unwilling to give her the satisfaction of firing me again, I started searching for another job.

After approximately a year, I transitioned to a job with Eagle Travel as a tour guide, only to stay for a month before securing a position at Zambia National Provident Fund, (ZNPF) in Lusaka as an Accounts Clerk. This move alleviated my parents' concerns. While at ZNPF, I decided to pursue further education and improve my Grade 12 certificate with the hope of getting into the University of Zambia.

During this period, Zambia Airways advertised positions for air stewards and stewardesses, and I applied, went through interviews, and successfully made it to the final shortlist.

Chapter 5
Encountering Destiny

Back at the reception of the Fairmount Hotel, I was engrossed in my work as two gentlemen were playing with one slot machine. It was obvious that they were winning some money from the noise of the coins gushing out of the machine. 'She looks like Gamma,' said one of them in trying to mimic an advertisement that was running on national television. In the advertisement, Gamma meant good. I was oblivious to the fact that they were trying to get my attention, so I carried on with my work. They were liaising with Arnold, a gentleman who I was doing the shift with. He told them we were scheduled to knock off at 22:00 hours, and they realized that they were out of time. The taller and darker of the two gentlemen advanced towards the reception and greeted me. We got talking, he asked my name, and he introduced himself. He explained that they came to lodge at Fairmount Hotel for the night, because they had missed their flight back to Lusaka after attending a pass-out parade, at the Zambia Air Force.

When they went back to reclaim their rooms at the Intercontinental Hotel, they found that the rooms had been sold, hence their decision to come to Fairmount Hotel. Somehow, our conversation revealed that I was scheduled to travel to Lusaka for an interview at Chainama College in a few days. It was a Friday, and we said our goodbyes because they were leaving the next morning.

The following Monday, I got a phone call from a lady at the Zambia Airways ticket sales office. She identified herself and asked to verify my full name and my intended travel dates to Lusaka, because she had an airline ticket for me. Perplexed by this utterance, I asked, "From who?" and she informed me it was from Lt. Col. Sande Kayumba at ZAF.

"What?" I thought he was joking when he passively made mention of it; I sighed to myself, "Me on an aeroplane," I sighed again. I had never been on an aeroplane in my life, but my desire to get on the plane to see exactly what the air hostesses did in mid-air, was the low-hanging fruit. I did not even know how to break this news to my parents as they were preparing me for a train ride. Should I tell them? One voice inside me asked, and the other voice answered, you have to. That part turned out easy because my brother Ben was also working for Zambia Airways, so it was easy to tell them that Ben bought the ticket for me. I connived with Ben, who agreed to cover me.

The next hurdle was how to get on the flight and not see the Colonel in Lusaka. At this time, my main interest was to see and have a feel of the plane ride, and see exactly how the air hostesses were working in the cabin. I convinced myself that I would somehow manage to escape from him upon landing. I got on the flight and arrived in Lusaka after one hour. I had no idea what the protocol was like at the airport as it was my first time.

The doors to the Hawker Siddeley 748 opened outwardly, and I took a walk to the rear exit in order to get down the stairs. As I looked down from the galley of the aircraft, I saw a figure of an Air Force officer waiting at the bottom of the stairs. He was medium to tall in height, with a chocolate complexion. He looked more handsome and majestic in his uniform. His body measurements looked perfect in every dimension, and his whole anatomy was quite exciting. I looked again, and yes, it was Sande looking totally different in uniform.

In my first encounter with him at the hotel, he was wearing casual clothes. I also had no idea that he had that much access to the airport ramp. No way out, I said to myself. He picked me up with his driver, took me to the mess for a drink, and then dropped me off at my sister Stella's place in Northmead."What have I just done? Now he even knows where I am staying?" I spoke to myself repeatedly. I confided in my sister about my move, and we started scheming.

In the morning, I attended the interview at Chainama College, and in the afternoon, we had agreed that Sande would send a driver to pick me up. Stella and I have a striking resemblance, so when the driver arrived to pick me up, we decided to confuse him by saying the person he came to pick up was another sister of ours who was not home. The driver believed us, and he left. Sande was angry with the driver, so they came back for me together, and we went for drinks again. Our ages were revealed in our discussion, and I discovered that he was nineteen years older than me. In his mind, he had found a partner, but for me, that was the deal breaker.

The next day, he took me to the airport, and I managed to fly back to Livingstone. From that day, he continued pursuing me without ceasing. He called me several times a day, which was inappropriate for someone manning a front office. Often, I would give the excuse that I was unable to speak with him, because my boss was close by, or that I was attending to customers. He still did not relent; he continued calling periodically, and we chatted briefly as I continued claiming I was too busy.

Along the way, I got a job with the Zambia National Provident Fund as an Accounts Clerk. This meant that I had to move to Lusaka. I started by staying with my cousin Loyce and her husband, Edwin. After a while I found myself staying at the Chelston Government flats with my elder cousin Panic Malawo, a lady captain ZAF officer. Panic was one of the graduates at the pass-out parade when Sande and his friend missed their flight. The guy he was playing the slot machines with was his best friend Christopher Chilufya, (Chris) who later married Panic. My stay with Panic quickly revealed my whereabouts to Sande. One day, he and Chris appeared at Panic's doorstep, much to my surprise, and the chase for me continued.

Through interactions, it was easy to tell that Sande was an extremely smart guy. He said he had just come out of a nasty divorce, and he was looking for a suitor. The idea of marriage just had me jumping out of my skin. I was just a kid, and naturally, I wanted to do the things that my fellow kids were doing, like clubbing and going to parties and discos. I think Sande sensed that, so he was very patient with me. Sometimes, he would arrive with Chris at Panic's flat, and while they chatted in the living room, I would find my way out of the flat, because I did not want to go out to dinner with them.

In my mind, dinners were for big people. I wanted to go to the Municipal Sports Club (Munis) with my brothers, where kids my age would hang out. The trio nicknamed me akasabi (small fish) because of my elusive nature. Each time I would do a disappearing act on them, I knew I was in trouble with Panic, who thought I was being stupid. Sande was patient with me because he allowed the kid in me to play. A few times, he would actually drop me, my friends, and my brothers at Valentinos, a disco house in the CBD, and would give us pocket money. Sometimes, he would even come to fetch us. He continued pursuing me for a long time, and after a few glasses of whisky, he always said to Chris, "The Vulture is a patient bird."

When nothing else seemed to work for Sande, he devised another plan. Squash. He used to play Squash with Chris at the British Petroleum Club in the show grounds, and they incorporated Panic into their team. Sande decided to entice me into playing Squash, and of course, I accepted because I liked it. I watched Panic's game improve and just loved how she looked in her Squash kit. His coaching efforts definitely won my heart on the court. He was patient when coaching me and was happy that my game improved so quickly. He travelled to the UK, and when he returned, he brought me a full squash kit. I loved this game so much, and he knew that if he wanted a date with me, it had to start with a game of squash. This carried on for some time until I started getting comfortable around him.

Chapter 6
Realizing the Skyward Dream

Mutinta as the face of Zambia Airways-1991.

I embarked on the eight-week cabin crew A.B. Initio Course in 1988, joining like-minded individuals at Zambia Airways. A.B. Initio was a course high on passenger safety and service proficiency on board an aircraft. The instructors were very clear from the onset. We were taught never to compromise on passenger safety; therefore, a 100% pass in emergency procedures was not negotiable for those aiming to go on the line. Even in my sleep, I could hear my instructor Marian's voice repeatedly warning the class about that. It was a do-or-die for me; getting in was difficult enough because there were over 300 applicants chasing after 40 jobs.

I was training to be an air hostess, so I was already feeling close to the line. Failing was not an option. I got to learn my emergency and service procedures and qualified to go on the line. Initially, I was trained on aircraft HS 748, ATR 42, and Boeing 737, which meant that I could only fly locally and regionally. It was not long before I converted to the McDonnell Douglas DC10 (Nkwazi), which was the airline's flagship plane. This meant that I could operate international flights.

My first international flight was to London; it was nine straight hours. It shattered all my glamorized expectations, revealing the manual labour and challenges behind the scenes. In my mind, this was to be a simple trip characterized by glam. Alas, early into the flight, I realized that behind the glam was a lot of hard work, often struggling to stay awake when you are on watch, and failing to sleep when you are assigned to rest.

This trip to England brought the truth to light; I realized that I was a glorified waiter, maybe one of the hardest jobs I have ever done in my life. With my service and emergency procedures in my head, I set out to do what I had always dreamt of doing when I was young. In spite of this rude awakening, I repeatedly told myself that no matter how hard it got, giving up was not an option.

Later, on the same flight to London, I got another rude shock. I operated as crew member No. 9 on the Nkwazi. The role of No. 9 on the flight was to be in charge of the bar. At that time, Zambia Airways only offered complimentary soft drinks, while all alcoholic drinks had to be paid for by passengers. I was to trust the other five crew members to collect money on my behalf, whenever they sold alcohol. However, at the end of the flight, I discovered that I had a shortage of seventy-one Pounds.

Due to the fact that we were six crew members on the service in the economy class cabin, it was practically impossible for me to point out who was dishonest, or may have neglected to collect the money from the passengers. In the de-brief session, I was too scared to bring it to my Purser's attention that I had run a shortage, for fear of being grounded. This meant that my allowance in London was already reduced by seventy-one Pounds.

Mutinta as
Miss Zambia Airways-1990.

From that rude awakening on my maiden international flight, going forward, I somehow managed to escape being in charge of the bar. It did not take very long before I was allocated a room at the Young Women's Christian Association, popularly known as the Y. I moved out of Panic's flat to share a room with Patricia Zimba. Bless her resting soul. She was so fun-loving, and we got on like a house on fire.

Two years into my job in 1990, I was informed that I had to take part in a mandatory cabin service contest to choose Miss Zambia Airways. Miss QZ was picked at a contest where one had to demonstrate exemplary service and safety procedures. The winner was to represent the airline in all its marketing campaigns and generally be the airline's face.

Growing up, I was a very timid person, and I thought this was too mammoth a task for me to undertake. I had ducked the 1989 contest, so this time around, there was no way out.

There were eleven other contestants, and our chaperons started preparing us for the contest. Naturally, all the contestants had to get off the flight schedules in order to make this happen. Miss Zambia Airways was an annual event that most Lusaka residents looked forward to, so, everything had to be on point.

The day of the contest came. The Hotel Intercontinental was the preferred venue for this pageant. The hotel was a hive of activity as we, the contestants, were up and about in the hotel lobby, trying everything to calm our nerves. Stanley Makulu, the master of ceremonies, was constantly teasing us all in an attempt to restore our fluctuating temperaments.

On my right is late former Minister of Transport and communications Brigadier General Enos Haimbe and on my left, is late former Managing Director for Zambia Airways Capt. Godfrey Mulundika.

The evening quickly arrived. I was contestant number four out of twelve. There were four judges, and my turn quickly came. Stan Max, as he would refer to himself, introduced me to the judges and the crowd. After thanking him, I welcomed the cheering crowd to the high-flying world of Zambia Airways. Even if I wore my best layer of confidence, I could feel my heart beating faster because of the stage fright. I said a short prayer, "Lord, I need you on my side this moment."

The judge asked me to serve a red wine, and I gave him a choice of the reds I had. A French Bordeaux or Beaujolais. I looked for the glass appropriate for red wine, and I made sure the wine was at room temperature, following the red wine etiquette. I poured a little for him to taste according to the wine service tradition. I saw a nod of approval on his face, signalling that he liked the wine." May I pour your drink, sir?" I heard myself asking. Another nod signalled that I could. Phew! That was my service contest done, and I knew that I had nailed it to the T.

The next round was the oral questions, centred around in-flight safety. My turn came sooner than I thought. Stan Max asked me to imagine I was on a plane taking off for Ndola, and I needed to make a safety briefing before takeoff. "Piece of cake," said my inner voice. I went through the safety announcement the best way I could do it, and when all was said and done, I felt like a winner. It was not possible to see how the others had fared in the contest, as we were all required to be backstage, while one of us was being tested. I left it all to the judges and ultimately to the Divine.

The wait was long and simply nerve-racking; one hour seemed like forever. I was in the dressing room with Christine, one of the contestants, and we were visibly gripped with anxiety. Failing to calm our nerves naturally, we found ourselves dipping into the chillers containing Don Perignon.

Later in the night, there was pin-drop silence in the south ballroom of the Hotel Intercontinental, as Stan Max returned to the catwalk. He started his preamble to the final announcement. After a round of jokes, he received the results from the judges. The winner of Miss Zambia Airways 1990 is… and quiet he went before he repeated in slow motion, "contestant number one, two, three" and rested firmly on contestant number four. I emerged from the dressing room to the catwalk, where I joined the Minister for Transport and Communication, the late Brigadier General Enos Haimbe, my Managing Director, the late Captain Godfrey Mulundika, and the reigning Miss Zambia Airways then, Josephine Chilufya Mukuka. She was to hand over the crown and trophy to me. The south ballroom was palpable with joy, as the crowd chanted, Mutinta! Mutinta! Mutinta! She put the sash over my shoulder, directed the two sides to meet at my left hip, and then handed the trophy to me. The sash was written "Miss Zambia Airways 1990." My inner voice said, "Thank you, Lord. I only asked to be an air hostess, and you gave me much more."

Gary and Mutinta in the New York Penta Hotel-New York.

My face adorned offices, billboards, television, magazines, brochures, newspapers, and various promotional materials both at home and abroad. My life went through a drastic change. I won a holiday trip for two to Kasaba Bay, a world-class resort on Lake Tanganyika in Zambia, and one of the deepest lakes in Africa.

I also won K15,000,000.00 (Fifteen million kwacha un-rebased) and $2000.00 (Two thousand United States dollars) and a holiday trip for two to the Bahamas Islands. I was assigned to help with all the marketing campaigns of the airline, and on most flights, I was elevated to operate from first class, which carried the Zambia Airways' highest customer segment. I was privileged to serve high-network and net-worth customers. On one of my flights, I was privileged to serve our first Republican President, Dr. Kenneth Kaunda, and later his counterpart, then President of Burundi, Mr. Pierre Buyoya.

Sande and Mutinta in Sbarro Pizza restaurant in NewYork.

I went off the roster to enable me to take my holidays. I chose to go to Kasaba Bay with Sande. We had reasonably bonded by this time, and he made it clear that he would not let me go. To make our relationship work, Sande had to knock off a few years from his age, and equally, I had to add a few years to my age. That way, we seemed to get on. Together with my chaperons, Hilary Fyfe and Malama Nsofwa, and my runner-up Catherine Mkandawire, we set out to go on our holiday.

Kasaba Bay was nice. Apart from the airline's organized tours, Sande taught me how to swim. After Kasaba Bay, I was to go to the Bahamas Islands. Gary and I had made a pact that if I won the pageant, I would travel with him. I was in a serious relationship with Sande, but I was also not about to disappoint Gary, because I knew what getting on an aeroplane to the Bahamas via New York meant for him. Sande was understanding about this, so he quickly suggested that he buy his own ticket to enable the three of us to travel together, and that was exactly what we did.

Gary left a week earlier, and we linked up with him in New York. By the time we got there, he already knew his way around. We toured New York. We went to see the Statue of Liberty, Times Square, and the Empire State Building, where we got a view of the city from the top. We toured the city which never sleeps, through the tall buildings and quickly identified eating places like the Sbarro, Tads Steak House, and a local pub called the Blarney Rock, where we used to have our drinks every evening. I was personally mesmerized by the organized yellow cabs queuing up for customers, the forever blaring horns, the graffiti on the walls, the free-spirited and dope-looking population.

In the Electronic Shop where we bought the TDK cassettes in New York.

I also got to learn what the older stewards and stewardesses were doing as side hustles. Buying and selling (Makwebo). At that point, it made sense for Gary and me not to proceed to the Bahamas Islands. We ended up buying suitcases and suitcases of TDK cassettes for resale. The abandoned Bahamas trip ushered me into the business world. As time went by, I started having regrets about abandoning the trip. The chance was in my hands, at no cost, but I let it slip away. I remained forever, longing to go to the Bahamas.

When Gary and I abandoned the trip to the Bahamas, we decided to buy TDK cassettes which filled the suitcases above. That was how I started business.

One of my roles as Miss Zambia Airways was to join the marketing team of the airline in promotional and marketing campaigns. Zambia Airways was particularly going through a re-branding exercise, which mainly involved the change of ladies' uniforms. Although it was an exciting process for us ladies, I did not understand why the airline changed the uniform, which represented the Zambian national flag. The uniform was changed to some blue and green striped uniforms with plain coloured blue and green Jackets.

In my view, the brand went through some inconsistency. All the equipment on the aeroplanes and the aircraft themselves had the consistency of the Zambian flag. However, I was too small in line to even sound this inconsistency to anyone. All of us female flying crew were scheduled to go to England for the fitting of our new uniforms, which we received soon after. It went without saying that the target markets had to be enlightened on this major change in the brand.

I, together with my runners-up, were subjected to a screen test to determine our suitability for a television commercial. I came out tops. I then had to travel to Harare, Zimbabwe, with the Zambia Airways Marketing Director, Mr. Bernard, for a whole week to shoot the advertisement. All that was in my sight that week were cameras and video machines, and people making me do the same things over and over again. I must admit that for a moment, it stopped being fun, and became monotonous.

Sande and I had settled into our relationship by this time. He would not let me go to Harare alone either, so he took leave from work and jumped on the bandwagon.

He has a friend in Harare who answers to the name Edward Berry (Ed). They arranged that when I was busy at work, he and Ed would go out chilling.

Sande and Ed first met at a time when they were both going through their divorce proceedings, and they vowed to each other that there would be no more marriages going forward. When I first met Ed, one evening after the shoot, Sande introduced me as Mutinta, and so Ed asked tauntingly, "Is she your Mrs?" Sande would not answer this question but only managed to make a facial expression, indicating that I was not. They had made a pact not to ever get married again, and Sande knew, but could not say to Ed, that he was about to break his side of the deal.

The television commercial hit the Zambian screens just before we were to get married. The little fame I had, was now amplified by the Zambia National Broadcasting Corporation. This celebrity status came with its own challenges. While I was easily recognized by most people, it was impossible for me to know everyone. As a result, the court of public opinion judged me harshly and labelled me a show-off. I was initially not aware that I was labelled that way, until a friend of mine mentioned it to me. At the time, she said that I was with Gary, who was already a prominent figure in the Zambian space. He said that he suffered the same judgment, so he made it a point that if someone made eye contact with him, he then said hello. I pondered to myself as to how, I would manage to constantly look in people's eyes as a woman. In order to distract this thought, I quickly focused on something else.

On the other hand, Sande saw the need to ring-fence my left third finger.

Sande teaching Mutinta how to swim while on holiday in Kasaba Bay.

Chapter 7
The Proposal

I was living at the YWCA Hostel when I won the pageant, and by that time, Sande was known to my friends and siblings. Every day after work, he came to the YWCA to pick me up for a meal or a chill. The Y, as we called it, had one funny rule, which prohibited entry after 22:00 hours in the night. I was the only exception to the rule because the airline negotiated with the matron for extended hours, as long as I was operating a late flight. Because of this, I enjoyed a bit more freedom compared to the other girls. Sande and I had fully bonded by this time. On some days, we could not make it back before the curfew, so I found myself at his place often.

My uncle Frank had a habit of randomly checking up on me at the Y. One morning, Sande dropped me at the hostel in order for me to get ready for my flight pick-up. The matron, who always called me by my surname, barged into my room and said, "Nkombo, your uncle has been coming to check on you, and you are simply never here. I have run out of excuses to cover for you."

Following that, one weekend, I checked in at Uncle Frank's house at No. 5 Mwapona Road in the Woodlands Suburb, so that he could see me. He was quick to say that I was never at the hostel because each time he came to see me, he bounced. I told him that being Miss Zambia Airways was demanding too much of my time, which was not entirely true. Sande was occupying the rest of the time that Zambia Airways was not. I was spending more and more time with Sande, and my wardrobe slowly started choking his wardrobe.

Many guys, especially the flying crew, tried their luck with me even when it was obvious that I was now officially taken by the Colonel from ZAF. A steward called David, who was in my elder brother Ben's intake, repeatedly teased me about going out with a soldier. In his mind, Sande was a typical soldier, and according to him, it was an inferior move. He continued making fun of this for the longest time.

On the other hand, Uncle Frank and I were now playing cat and mouse. He caught wind of the fact that I was going out with Sande, and he summoned me to his house. He said to me that he had received reports that I was no longer found at the hostel. "How does he get to know all these things?" I asked myself.

My father also joined his brother in conducting snap checks via telephone. Each time he called, I was not there, but it was always easy to say I was working. Clearly, I was under pressure, and the only solution was to get back to the hostel, where I now had a skeleton wardrobe. I shared my predicament with Sande and told him that I had to start spending more time at the hostel.

Luckily for me, Zambia Airways gave me a flat in the Northmead area of Lusaka. As Miss Zambia Airways, I was entitled to decent accommodation. While preparing to move to my flat, Sande proposed to his cousin Humphrey Mulemba, to take the traditional plates to Uncle Frank to ask for my hand in marriage. That was how the marriage proposal came, and I agreed.

The inner child in me looked forward to him kneeling down with flowers and a ring in his hand, but this did not happen because Sande is a very traditional man. The inner parent in me said, "Do not sweat the small stuff, Mutinta." I focused on the bigger picture, walking down the aisle with military honours.

This process all happened very quickly, and I did not have a chance to enjoy my youth, let alone live in my own flat. I ended up letting my brother Gary, who had just gotten married to his childhood sweetheart Katendi, and my sisters Nchimunya, Cholwe, and Nachilala live in my flat until I had to surrender it back to the airline.

Chapter 8
Embracing New Beginnings

Mr. Humphrey Mulemba, like Uncle Frank, was also a very senior Politician in the first Zambian Republic, so the two knew each other very well and were basically peers. He made the trip to No. 5 Mwapona Road, to take the traditional plates to signify that they had identified a potential bride in that household. Uncle Frank called me to verify whether I knew Col. Sande Kayumba and if we had plans for marriage. I confirmed that I knew him and that we had plans to get married. All the formalities were done, and the bride price was paid.

Following the pre-marital rituals, my days were full of activity as I was preparing for my wedding. It was 1991, the year of the revolution, when Zambia was going to have its first-ever multiparty elections. The country was upbeat, and every corner was screaming, "The hour has come." President Kenneth Kaunda was, for the first time, going to be challenged by a human being and not the usual frog symbol that he paraded on the ballot paper, as his opponent.

We had just come out of two weddings in the family, for Ben and Margaret on June 30th and Gary and Katendi on August 31st, and mine was set for 19th October of the same year. Clearly, my parents were overwhelmed, so they tried to postpone my wedding to the next year on account of having no more money. This did not sit well with Sande, who could not wait any longer. He cooked up a story that he was to be posted out of the country, hence the reason for his rush. He also said he was equal to the huge task and cost of the wedding. We started our preparations.Sande and I agreed that we were going to have a military wedding.

He and his groomsmen planned our wedding like a military operation order according to the Air Force tradition. They came up with an operation order code-named "Kabwendo." They called themselves the friendly forces, and referred to me and my bridesmaids as the enemy forces. Their mission was to capture "the highly sophisticated devious enemy commander," Mutinta, and the capture was to happen at the Civic Centre, to be followed by a celebration of the successful capture at the Chamba Valley Officers' Mess.

The days prior to the wedding were exciting. Obviously, I took leave to prepare for my nuptials. There were two people who I wanted to be part of my wedding line-up: Gary and my cousin Machila Malawo. Unfortunately, they could not, simply because they were not military officers.

My bridesmaids consisted of a friend I met at Zambia Airways Training School, Jacqui, my sisters Nchimunya and Cholwe, and my cousin Panic. Sande's groomsmen were Colonels in the ZAF, his best friend Christopher Chilufya, Christopher Singogo, Peter Mulasikwanda, and Mas Musonda. Military etiquette demanded the line-up to be supported by officers of the rank of Major as swordsmen.

For my special day, I picked Petronella Thomas, (Petty) to serve as my matron. Petty was one lady whose style I admired from way back in Livingstone, and one who typically saw me grow up. Petty and my cousin Gertrude Katandula, who were best of friends, organized, and hosted my bridal shower, where I got gifts to start my new kitchen. Saturday morning of 19th October 1991, finally arrived! My bridesmaids and I went to dress up from my Uncle Frank's house.

My maid of honour, Jacqui, ensured I wore something new, something old, something blue, and something borrowed.

Our wedding day photo session at the Goma Lakes in Lusaka.

My matron did my makeup, and my bridesmaids helped me get into my beautiful wedding gown, which I bought from Debenhams on one of my trips to London.

A fleet of decorated cars was parked outside Uncle Frank's house, waiting to deliver the enemy commander and the enemy forces to the Civic Centre. Back in the living room, the elders prayed for safe passage and for the best outcomes all around. I was taken to the waiting Mercedes Benz, where I sat with my left hand sandwiched by my father's two hands. I wished he could tell me what he was going through.

We drove to the Civic Center, where the friendly forces and their swordsmen were waiting to capture. My father walked me down the aisle, assisted by relatives singing the famous Londo-losela Tonga marriage chorus. The marriage presiding officer took us through our vows, and called for the rings. Jacqui and I had taken a trip to England, where we chose the ring from the H Samuel Store in Holborn, London, and Sande's friend Stephen Muson'a, met us there and paid for it.

In no time, we were pronounced husband and wife. More choruses followed the vows as we walked out of the Civic Centre to file through clashing military swords, drawn into an arc. By all standards, it was a very colourful event, and I knew I had scored a first in the family. The marriage ceremony was followed by a wedding celebration at the Chamba Valley Officers' Mess. My situation shifted once again, and I was now to answer to the name Mutinta Nkombo-Kayumba.

Sande did not invite Ed to the wedding for a known reason; he had broken his side of the deal. And when Ed later found out that we were married, Sande laboured to justify why he broke his end of the deal. He repeatedly said to him, "She is an air hostess, Ed." To this day, Ed jokes that he will stay single unless he meets an air hostess. Three decades later, we are all still searching for an air hostess for Ed.

Through my marriage, I made great friendships that outlived my marriage, such as Irene Muson'a, who has become my big sister, friend, and spiritual mentor. She came along with her childhood friend Prisca Matimba, who has also impacted my life positively. Other friends whom I met through my marriage are Kinah Simbeye and Christine Sakala.

We were oriented as military wives at totally different intervals. We took some liking for one another, and our friendship grew. Christine was married to Sande's late friend Cuthbert Sakala. Christine is a free-spirited, loving soul. Together with her, Gary, Katendi, and myself, we took a road trip to Johannesburg to watch a football match between Zambia and South Africa. We had so much fun, most of which was away from the stadium.

As a result, the return trip was hectic, because we drove through the night. Gary, who was the primary driver, decided to take a short nap to recharge. Katendi thought she would save us time by continuing to drive. The three of us slept, and when Gary opened his eyes, it was dawn, and he realized that we were driving through some unfamiliar landscape, with no road signs and markings. Upon enquiry from the pedestrians, we realized we were heading towards Mozambique. Katendi had missed the turn, which would later take us to Zambia. The drive was exceptionally long, our budget was tight, and the fuel gauge was leaning towards red. We imagined another night on the road side, but by the grace of God we made it to the next gas station. However, we had so much fun as Christine continued to make us roll with laughter.

Chapter 9
Welcoming the Two Stars in My Life

After I got married, I continued flying and selling the airline. The advertisement would be aired several times a day on national television. Zambia Airways had exposed me to the finer things in life. I travelled the world through my job and my own personal escapades. I hit five continents before I turned thirty.

With my children Mwaji and Mashuta at Buffalo House along Independence Avenue Lusaka.

Soon after I got married, I was slowed down by pregnancy. I was expecting my first child. I went through my pregnancy with ease, no cravings or morning sickness. I was just shocked at the hormonal change my body went through. I grew so big and was worried that I would not manage to get back to my usual self. I went into the labour ward two weeks after my delivery due date. My doctor, Velepi Mtonga, advised that I had to be induced.

At the previous ante-natal visit, a check revealed that the fluid in my tummy was Meconium-stained, which meant that any further delay would distress my baby.

I was induced at 17:00 hours on the 20th of July 1992, and was in intense labour for 24 hours. I had looked forward to a normal delivery and tried by all means to practice all the pre-delivery exercises I had read about. I was overly prepared. I had my mother-to-be hairstyle, which was to last for months, done by a Congolese stylist. Everything was new, including my fancy nightwear, and the Mother Care ensemble, in readiness for the arrival of my baby.

When the nurse came to do a check on me, she said my composure signalled that I was still far away from delivery. It did not take long after I was induced before I felt this excruciating pain. It was constant, severe, and simply dreadful. I could not equate it to any pain I had ever felt before. I cried out for my mother, and at other intervals, I cried out for Velepi. The midwife was not happy that I was crying for my doctor to help. Obviously, she didn't know that Velepi and I had reasonably bonded by then.

One by one, I started losing my fancy maternity clothes, and the nurses nodded, saying, "Yes, it is now time." And when it was time to push out the baby exactly 24 hours later, I struggled to push and failed, much to Velepi's anger. I had not eaten anything; the only thing I had in my system was the syntocinon, which made me jump around like a headless chicken. By the time the critical moment to deliver arrived, I had no energy left to bring anyone to life.

Velepi was visibly angry with me and repeatedly accused me of wasting away contractions. From that very charming doctor, her voice shifted with authority to a do-or-die tone. She tried all sorts of instructions, but it didn't work. Scared that I would lose the baby, she went ahead and delivered the baby using a vacuum extractor. Mwaji was born. My bouncy baby girl, weighing 4 kilograms, was immediately attached to my tummy for a bonding session. When all was said and done, Velepi came back to my bedside, with the most captivating smile and asked, "Are we still friends?" And I murmured, 'Yes, yes.'

I went back to work after five months. I was now a mother. The most difficult thing was to fly away for days and leave my baby with my sisters, Nchimunya, Cholwe, my late niece Doreen, and her nanny Idah. Even if I seemed to have created an army of people against one Mwaji, every trip I undertook was filled with guilt. No amount of sterling pounds would make up for the guilt I would carry with me to and from London. Not even the shopping would take away the guilty feeling.

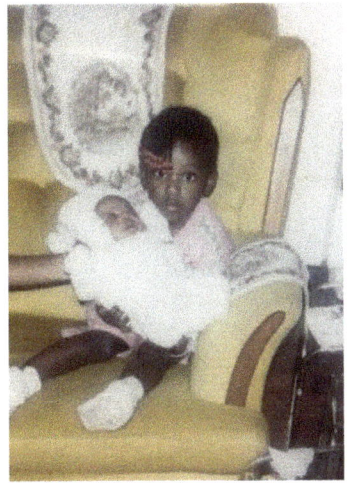

Mwaji at 3 years old with her baby brother Mashuta-1995.

In 1995, exactly three years later, and in July again, Velepi and I found ourselves in the labour ward. It seemed like a copy-and-paste action. I went over 40 weeks into pregnancy, and I had to be induced again. The labour pattern was not any different from the first one. When I was fully dilated, Velepi did not waste time. She delivered my second baby with a vacuum extractor once again. My son Mashuta was born, a bouncy baby weighing 3.5 kilograms.

Velepi tried to explain to me the reason why I could not have a normal delivery in medical terms; I could not be bothered much because I told myself that was my last trip to the labour ward. I had a girl and a boy; what more could a girl ask for?

At the top of the Table Mountain in Cape Town South Africa with my son Mashuta-2021.

Chapter 10
Grounded Dreams: "The Closure of Zambia Airways"

It was the year 1993. It became apparent that Zambia Airways had to go through some restructuring as it was not making profits. One gloomy morning, a press release confirmed that Zambia Airways was faced with huge financial stress, and therefore, could not avoid a retrenchment exercise. Every one of us, from the ground staff to the flying crew, was anxious, constantly wondering whether our names were on the retrenchment list or not.

One day after a flight, I found a note in my pigeonhole asking me to see our In-flight Service Manager. I went to his office only to be handed a brown envelope. We had heard that brown envelopes had started flying around. I knew before I read what was in the envelope, that I had been retrenched. I was young, naive, and very oblivious to the power I held as Miss Zambia Airways.

I went home and told my family that I had been retrenched. I was helpless and simply did not know what to do with myself. My sister-in-law, Gary's wife Katendi, could not stomach that either. Katendi is sleek, medium height, with an espresso complexion, and a firm believer in human rights. She came to me and fed me with all sorts of ideas of how I was to fight for my job back. She was not motivated by my lukewarm response. I thought whatever she was saying would be impossible. The letter was in my hands, and the signature of the Human Resource Director (HRD) was already on it, so as far as I was concerned, it was over.

She used her wisdom to confide in her late father, Honourable Paul Kapin'a, who was the then Minister of Community Development and Social Welfare, about my situation.

My Zambia Airways advertisement was still being aired by the national broadcaster. One day after the advertisement was aired on television, her father picked up the phone and called the then Minister of Transport and Communication, and said to him. "Minister, you retrench someone in the morning, and in the evening, you are using them to sell your airline," and the minister replied with a "How so?"

Honourable Kapin'a went ahead and explained my issue to him. The minister affirmed that it was a huge oversight, and that it could have been propelled by some malicious individual or someone who wanted to satisfy their personal and selfish needs. He promised that he would look into my issue the very next day. Katendi did all this behind my back, and when she was sure that she had holistically done her homework, she instructed me to go and see the Human Resources Director at Ndeke House, the head office.

By the time I got there, the HRD had already been briefed, and he, in turn, had briefed Flight Operations to put me back on the roster. I went back on the line without knowing who had maliciously put my name on the retrenchment list. I obviously trod very carefully from then onwards. I worked with different people on different flights, and I did not know when I was working with the enemy, so I had to execute my duties in an exemplary manner. Someone in a position of authority put my name on the retrenchment list to dim my light. I never got to know who it was.

What I knew for sure was that I had to constantly look everywhere: the front, the back, and my sides. I worked diligently and did not give anyone a chance to find fault in me.

Sadly, in 1994, it was announced on national television that the DC 10 aircraft was confiscated on arrival at London Heathrow Airport by the owners. This immediately crippled the airline, because the DC10 was the flagship aircraft for Zambia Airways, and literally the cash cow. This and many other reasons marked the sad end of the high-flying world of Zambia Airways.

My journey at Zambia Airways, like that of many others, ended abruptly, and I was officially unemployed.

Chapter 11
Daring the Business Skies

Shortly after Zambia Airways closed, I quickly had to start thinking of finding something to do for a living. During my time at Zambia Airways, I put away all plans to further my education, so I had no qualifications to lean on. I became a stay-at-home mother, and it was clear that staying at home did not do me any good.

Together with Sande and my brothers Ben and Gary, we pooled resources and decided to open a clothing store. That is how Candice Exclusive was birthed, on Cha Cha Cha Road in the CBD of Lusaka. By this time, I had realized my passion for fashion. Through the shopping experiences that I had undertaken while at Zambia Airways, I realized that I could effortlessly identify top fashion trends. I decided to use this strength for profit. At Candice Exclusive, we stocked apparel for both ladies and gentlemen, which we sourced from England, the United States of America, and Thailand.

There was ease of entry into this industry, and the Zambian Kwacha was relatively strong against major currencies, so it was easy to re-sale our merchandise. After trading for almost one year, we managed to secure a shop at Society Business Park on Cairo Road. With time, we realized that our decision-making process was slowed down, because we were too many. Apart from that, we were all married, so we decided to part ways so that we could work as independent couples, which made a lot of sense.

Sande and I decided to open our own shop. I sold my shares at Candice Exclusive, which formed part of my equity at Genuine Collections, a partnership we formed in 1998. This shop is located on the ground floor of Wood Gate House in the CBD, where we still trade today. Managing Genuine Collections kept me busy. Inevitably, I had to fly in and out of the country for re-stocking purposes.

One day, my husband who was commander of the Air Force, raised a concern which he said was coming from the system that employed him. The concern was that it did not augur well for me as commander's wife to continue flying around the world doing business. It seemed the idea of a commander's wife travelling with so many suitcases across many airports was not acceptable. He bought into the idea and advised me that quitting the business was the best for us. I resisted for a long time as I was very passionate about my work. It was not just part of my identity but also a source of livelihood for our family.

The idea of stopping work was killing me inside. I believed the pressure on my husband was coming from the common cultural belief at the time that, a woman's place was in the kitchen. I struggled with that notion, as my mother taught me that girls have so much to offer the world, both at home and in industry. So, I pleaded with my husband for me to continue with my work as it supplemented the family income.

However, I offered a concession, that if I would reduce the frequency of my international travel, then I would ask my brother Ben to help. He would offload and clear my many suitcases on arrival, while I was whisked away through the VIP lounge by Air force security personnel.

That method worked very well, as my husband agreed with my proposal, and I managed to reduce the frequency of my trips from four times to twice a year. I am very grateful today that my husband agreed to the concession, a privilege that many working women, married to high profile people, did not have, and may still not enjoy today.

My cousin Chimuka Malawo (Chim) was visiting Zambia from the UK at some point. Chim has medium height with a tawny complexion. Chim carries a head with a business mind; she encouraged me to explore the Turkish fabric market. She was then dating an Army officer, Pascal, who had had a long stint in Istanbul. He told Chim to advise me to explore this route, which seemed like it had never been travelled by many Zambian business people.

On another note, my friend Laura Kapihya, also from London, told me about her Turkish neighbour Simra, who would bring quality clothes and handbags whenever she visited her hometown, Istanbul. Laura is tall, slender, light-skinned and a natural with numbers. With this information on my hands, I started entertaining the idea of going to Turkey. I asked Laura to ask Simra to organize someone to take me around Istanbul, while I was there. Simra agreed. I then applied for a Turkish visa, which was issued out of Pretoria, South Africa.

As I set out for Istanbul, I was very scared but determined to succeed. I arrived at Attaturk International Airport in Istanbul, and was met by Simra's brother Faizal, who could hardly speak a word of English. I got even more scared when I discovered that almost all the people could not actually speak English at all. Even if Faizal was with me, I felt very much alone, and the feeling of fear prevailed almost always.

Communication between Faizal and myself was limited to Mutinta - Otel, meaning hotel, Mutinta - taxi, Mutinta - food, and so on and so forth.

Faizal took me to the wholesalers in Osmanbey, which is a typical garment district. There, I saw the beautiful merchandise through the beautifully decorated window displays. Finally, I had broken into a lucrative market. The prices were very affordable too. I tried to ask Faizal if he knew of a freight company to transport my goods to Lusaka, but he could not understand me at all. Even sign language failed to work. Back in the shops, I had a rude shock. Whenever I tried to pick out fast-selling sizes, the shopkeepers would go, "Yok! Yok! Yok! Series only," meaning "No! No! No! You have to buy the whole size run."

At this point, I didn't have much money to invest in the series method of buying; besides, there was uncertainty about how I would transport the goods to Zambia in time for Christmas. I didn't think it was wise to spend money in Turkey. Frustrated with everything not working out, I abandoned Turkey and took a flight to New York, where everything was familiar. But I knew because of what I saw, that I had to go back to Turkey again.

On another note, the trip to Turkey was quite intriguing. I learned quite a lot about the country's culture, mainly through observation. Turkey is a Muslim country. It was surprising to notice that every so often, people would abandon everything they were doing, to gather on the street to conduct their prayers in the open air. Something else that was very striking, was the generous nature of the Turkish people. Every shop we entered, offered us some food and drink.

By this time, my brothers and I had fully separated, and were managing our businesses independently. Even though we were managing separate shops, we assisted each other with contacts and generally still collaborated on anything to do with the business. After my return from Turkey, I briefed Gary about the challenges I experienced. He really cackled at the fact that language was the biggest barrier I faced in Turkey, and in his mind, he could have handled it better than me. After Christmas, we prepared to travel back to Istanbul on a fact-finding mission. When we got there, we booked into a hotel in an area called Sultana Ahmet with the help of the airport holiday booths.

Early the next morning, I was getting ready to go exploring. Gary got ready faster than me, so he left his room and went on the streets to test the waters. We later met at the breakfast table, where he confessed that he attempted to talk to some guys on the street, but they just looked and laughed at him. Several other attempts to engage people in the shops also proved futile. He had a taste of Istanbul too.

Convinced that we would not achieve anything, we started thinking about what to do, and where to go next. Our minds led us to the British Airways offices. Our thinking was that being an English airline, we were likely to find someone who spoke English there. We were right. We were given the phone number of one Mehmet, who was in the business of clearing and forwarding.

As if the British Airways staff knew, Mehmet could speak some bit of English. Mehmet owned a company called Met Cargo, and he agreed to not only forward our cargo but also take us around, and do some translation at a fee. We were also ready to shop using the method of series.

It was at this time that my business started making some sense. We comfortably went back and forth to Turkey before many Zambian business people knew about this market.

By the time many Zambians caught up, we were notches higher than the competition. Each time we went to Turkey, we engaged Mehmet, and he diligently helped us, especially with the translation. One day, we entered one shop, and the shop owner, who could speak a little bit of English, asked us why we always moved around with Mehmet. We replied that it was because of the language barrier. It was at that point that he told us that Mehmet was asking for a markup on everything we were buying, which made our goods expensive.

The next time we went to Turkey, we made sure we did not get in touch with Mehmet. We could count from one up to ten, in the Turkish Language, and we had learnt the names of colours too. We could also speak and understand some basics of the Turkish language by then, which was enough for us to get by. With a bit of the Turkish language on our tongues, we identified another shipper.

Before then, my friend Laura and I were trading in photographic paper. We invested equal amounts of money. Laura identified a source for photographic paper from England, which she would freight to Zambia, and I would receive, clear customs, and supply. We had a standing order with a photo Studio in the CBD, where we offloaded this paper. We made several rounds in supplying this paper, which made us some money.

I was then motivated to buy a property on Great East Road, which I later converted and ran as a guest house. Soon after I acquired this property, a friend of mine, Lanette Chiti, told me that she had a group of people coming to Zambia, and that they needed accommodation. Lanette is of medium height, slim, with a chocolate brown complexion. She mentioned that her guests wanted to stay in a home, and not a hotel. I quickly furnished the house to a good standard. The guests came and stayed at my house. They loved the place. However, being the first occupants, we discovered together that there were so many things wrong in the house. With very little knowledge of construction, Lanette and I tried to bring the best service providers to correct the mess. The tenants teased us repeatedly that we were learning to cut hair on a bald head.

After that, Zambia had an ad hoc demand for accommodation. This was shortly before the eclipse of the sun in 2001. Zambia was reported as one of the potential spots to provide a good view. Because of this, all roads led to Lusaka. Accommodation became scarce in the city. Some savvy Lusaka residents turned their homes into mini lodges and minted some money.

Fortunately, I was also able to pick up some guests who came for the solar eclipse, which took place on 21st June 2001. The same year, there was the International Conference on AIDS and STIs in Africa (ICASA) in Livingstone. As guests passed through Lusaka to Livingstone, I bagged some business as well. After that, the house was fully furnished and functional, and without any market research, I decided to open the house as a guest house. I called it Comfort Lodge.

There were no strict barriers to entry in this industry. It was also apparent that there was a gap that needed to be filled in the market. There was no accommodation for the business middle class as hotels were often too expensive or too cheap. The establishment of Comfort Lodge was one of the measures that closed this gap, because it was affordable and comfortable.

I entered the market and was proudly among the pioneers in the guest house business in Zambia. I assembled a team of workers to help me run the lodge. Its strategic location on the Great East Road highway gave us a competitive advantage over others. The lodge business thrived for some time. It transitioned through the stages of the product life cycle model very steadily, until it became apparent that the market was saturated. It was, however, a difficult business to run compared to the shop because it was hands-on, and it took a lot of my time and energy. The difference with the boutique business was that the lodge was selling an intangible service, and I trusted my workers for the service delivery almost always. Being a married woman with children, I was not able to be there all the time. Sometimes, I received messages complimenting the service, and other times, I was massaging customers' egos when they were dissatisfied.

The liberalized economy introduced by the New Deal government of President Frederick Chiluba brought about a lot of economic activities. Many more lodges suddenly mushroomed in Lusaka, saturating the market. While there seemed to be some expansion in the economy, a new problem set in, especially for my clothing business, there was an influx of people trading from the town centre where Genuine Collections is located.

This caused some congestion in the CBD. Shortly after that, the concept of malls was introduced in Zambia, which saw the opening of the Manda Hill Mall.

We started experiencing low sales in the CBD as most people shunned the town centre. For me to survive, I had to start thinking outside the box. I came up with the idea to open a shop at Comfort Lodge, thus pioneering the residential boutique concept, by setting up a shop within the premises. This was another first! It was unheard of to set up shop in a residential area.

I built a shop within the lodge premises, and to create awareness for the new outlet, I organized a launch graced by a man of God, Reverend Nashey. Often, people asked me who the customer would be away from town, but I knew that I had set up my own challenge to create a customer, and I did. The launch was very successful; the shop provided convenience for customers in the east of Lusaka, whose response was overwhelming. The fact that I was trading from my own space, gave me the liberty to keep the outlet open until late, to match the lodge's operating hours. This was another success story.

Along the way, I suffered a major setback; one day when I walked into the consular office of the American Embassy, and my visa was denied. I felt some sense of doom because America was my main source of ladies' clothing and Turkey for men. Inevitably, I discovered Italy, which became the preferred destination for shoes and handbags. I stayed without an American Visa for exactly ten years. This undoubtedly had a negative impact on my business. I had to do with Italy, the UK, and Turkey.

I then decided to join the American Chamber of Commerce in Zambia. The Chamber's main objective is to promote and facilitate trade partnerships and alliances between Zambian and American businesses. In August 2012, the chamber announced that there was going to be a show of American clothing brands in Las Vegas, Nevada, at the Magic Market Place. I expressed interest in attending this show. I applied for my visa again, and it was granted after a ten-year ban.

I was nominated to lead 12 women business leaders to the show. While there, we were introduced to famous American brands, and we met and networked with business leaders in the fabric market. The contacts created there have continued to be of use to my business to date.

It did not take very long after this; I identified another opportunity for market development. In 1997, I acquired a property in the Woodlands suburb, with a road frontage on Mwapona Road. It was a typical government house but with a big plot. Initially, the property was part of my real estate business portfolio. In 2016, I came up with the idea to divide it into two, leave the original house intact, and use the remaining extent to build a shop to add to the Genuine portfolio. The business was making more sense in the suburbs than in the town centre. After building and setting up, the outlet was ready for opening. I planned the official opening for 7th October 2017.

I again decided to create awareness for the outlet by running advertisements in the newspapers. Before then, I walked into the office of the then Ambassador of the United States of America to Zambia, Mr. Eric Shultz, and requested him to officially open the outlet.

He gracefully accepted my request, and said he was going to do it as one of his last assignments, as he was towards the end of his tour of duty in Zambia. At a colourful ceremony, he emphasized how pleased he was, to officially open an outlet carrying American merchandise.

Later in 2019, I was again privileged to join the President for Business and Professional Women, Rose Sibisi, and three other ladies, Maria Karima, Barbara Kamanga, and Effie Bwembya, at a women's conference in Egypt.

It was the Africa Conference of the International Federation of Business and Professional Women, in collaboration with Africa fashion reception, held under the theme, "Economic Empowerment & Entrepreneurship Promotion for Women," at the Conrad Hotel, Cairo, Egypt. We arrived at Cairo International Airport to a very warm welcome. The Zambian Ambassador to Egypt sent transport to take us to the Conrad Hotel. It was a two-day conference, and Africa had great representation from more than ten countries. After the conference, there was a fashion show where different countries showcased their cultures through dress, dance, and music. We showed off our Zambian flag, and also introduced some Zambian tunes to the eager crowd. After the two-day conference, the Ambassador also arranged for us to visit one of the Seven Wonders of the World, the Giza Pyramids. We shared quality time and space with the group members; we quickly bonded and called ourselves the "Egypt Bellas."

Covid 19 crept into Zambia in the year 2020. Businesses could not thrive as the Government urged people to stay at home. It was impossible to survive without customers. My business was not spared either. It made sense for me to scale down.

I went to the labour office to seek guidelines on the redundancy packages for my workers. Sadly, all operations at Comfort Lodge, including the boutique, had to shut down in August 2020, but I carried on running the remaining boutiques in the CBD, and the Woodlands suburb.

My business story cannot be told without mentioning my cousin, Eunice Hachipola, who is my strong right arm. She started working with me as a sales lady from inception in 1998, and to date, she has grown the business. Her loyalty, diligence, and trustworthiness remain unmatched. I had so many workers; some fell off in a nice way, and others on disciplinary and court charges. To date, Eunice has maintained her diligence as she is now the Group Manager.

Official opening of Genuine Outfitters by His Excellency Eric Schultz, Ambassador of the United States of America to Zambia-7th October 2017.

Chapter 12
Love in Uniform

Sande and Mutinta at the Zambia Air Force Annual Ball

My husband is an ex-military man who was trained as an Aeronautical Engineer at the University of Shrivenham in the United Kingdom. He rose through the ranks and became Commander of the Zambia Air Force in 1997. Before then, he attended the University of Zambia and Solwezi Secondary School in Northwest Zambia. Along the way, he acquired many qualifications, military decorations, and honours. One thing we liked doing together was playing squash and having drinks later. However, this did not last forever.

There was a failed attempted military coup in 1997 in Zambia. The announcement that a Captain in the Zambia Army had taken over the country came through our bedside radio. We lived on Independence Avenue, right opposite the State House of Zambia. Sande was a senior officer in the force, and in my mind, the coup plotters would come for us too. While the coup was in force, Sande took a stroll into the dressing room. I could hear that he was having a conversation with someone on the phone. This action did not give me any assurance that he was doing something about me and the children's safety. I found myself sweating profusely.

Although I felt more helpless than strong, I was still able to come up with a plan for safety.

I jumped out of bed, reached out for my tracksuit and trainers, put on a waist bag, and stashed it with all the money I had in the house. I put Mashuta on my back, strapped him with the famous Zambian baby wrap (Chitenge), and held Mwaji's hand, with plans of taking us somewhere safe. I had no idea where that would be, but my survival instincts led me to take that course of action. I stood in the bedroom for a long time, with sporadic thoughts of where would be the safest place.

As I was still contemplating my next move, Sande emerged from the dressing room, clad in his uniform. "You are crazy!" I said to him. "You can't possibly go out with what is going on out there." I forgot that it was no longer about his family, but the nation at large. He swore to defend the Constitution, the country, and its people.

Earlier on, I had heard him talking on the phone with the then Deputy Air Force Commander. The Deputy Air Force Commander lived three houses away from us in a double-storey house. He had the upstairs advantage for that purpose; he was updating Sande on the activity he was seeing on the road. Sande ordered me not to go anywhere.

Convinced that he could handle whatever was on the road, he got into his one-star dressed Toyota Cressida, registration number ZAF 3B, and wormed his way to ZAF Headquarters in Longacres. Within a few hours, he called to say the coup had been thwarted, and everything was okay, but he had to stay at work for the rest of the day. Despite the assurance that the situation had returned to normal, I was still tripping, and my mood was only restored when he returned home very late that evening.

I was looking forward to hearing exactly what had happened, but his training did not allow him to share anything with me. Shortly after the attempted coup, he was appointed Commander of the Zambia Air Force. We moved to the official residence of the Air Force Commander, also known as Air House. Sande suddenly got busy, and our time together got limited. We could no longer play squash together, although he was sometimes able to play during lunch breaks, depending on his schedule.

As a businesswoman and mother with two young children, I was also busy. As Commander's wife, I had to assume the role of patron for the Air Power Ladies Club. This was an organization formed to foster good relationships among wives of military personnel; it also kept me busy. The result of these engagements, unfortunately, created a distance in our relationship. However, the official engagements always brought us back together.

Sande's job sometimes required him to travel. On some visits, he was required to travel with me. Among the visits we undertook together was the tour of the South African Air Force bases. This trip has remained vivid in my mind because we connected well with our hosts. It was 11th September 2001, on his birthday, and I had made a prior arrangement with his friends Jammie and Burkey to give him a birthday dinner on arrival.

We flew to Johannesburg with his support staff only to arrive with the news breaking that the American Twin Towers were invaded. Our spirits were dampened about the loss of lives that happened there.

However, we proceeded with our dinner, which went very well. The next morning, work began for him. While Sande was working, the South African Air Force commander's wife, and some ladies of staff officers took me for a tour of the glass factory. Thereafter lunch was hosted in my honour at the Garden World Complex. In the evening, I had the pleasure of meeting with the South African Air Force (SAAF) Commander, at a dinner organized in our honour, at the Waterkloof base.

With the Air Force Commander of Uruguay and his wife.

The next day, we were taken on a helicopter ride to Robben Island, to see the cell where the legendary Nelson Mandela was held for years. We were also treated to an aerial view of Table Mountain in an Oryx helicopter, and after that, we had dinner at the Butcher Shop and Grill restaurant. It was my first time to visit Cape Town.

I could see that it was a nice place, but our visit was short and guarded. I wished I had more time and freedom to explore on my own, but we had to head back home after four nights.

Inside the cell of the legendary Nelson Mandela, former President of the Republic of South Africa.

On another trip, we visited Montevideo in Uruguay, where Sande was the only African Commander invited to a conference for Commanders of the Americas. The visit was a wonderful opportunity for the Commanders and their spouses to network and get to know each other. A lot of activities were arranged for spouses while the Commanders conferred. We were allocated some time to shop as well.

On the eve of our departure, we were all driven in a sixty-seater luxury bus for dinner. In the military, seniority is the buzzword, so we waited for our turn to get out of the bus. I noticed that all the Commanders came out of the bus, and immediately locked their hands with those of their spouses, and made grand entrances into the banquet hall. We were the odd couple in Montevideo. We did not hold hands but just walked side by side, a typical Zambian couple in Montevideo.

In Zambia, it is uncommon for couples to hold hands, and when they do, it is mostly perceived as a weakness on the part of the man. However, the dinner and the whole trip, in general, were still very enjoyable.

The visit to China was the longest of all the trips we had undertaken. We braved a fierce winter to tour some Chinese cities, namely Xian, Zhuhai, Schenzhen, Shanghai, and Beijing. We got to visit some aircraft manufacturers there. What I remember the most about this trip was that we drove for many hours through snowy conditions, and because of this, I sometimes opted to stay away or remain in the car.

Our visit to China.

Lots of lunches and dinners were lined up after each activity, and we were not spared from the famous Chinese toast, the "Ganbei." The highlight of this trip was being taken to see the iconic Great Wall of China in Beijing. Being there was a good feeling, although we failed to get to the top, because of the extreme weather conditions. I wished we had taken this trip when the weather was a bit friendlier, but we could not dictate as we were invitees.

The last trip we took together was to Brazil in 2002. Our itinerary read, Lusaka-London-Brasilia-SaoPaulo-Rio-de-Janeiro and back the same way to Zambia. It was the very last trip, and notably different from all the other trips we had undertaken. We departed from Lusaka International Airport with the full decorum that characterizes the departure of a Commander in ZAF.

We arrived to another warm welcome in Brasilia. Brasilia was nice; I had my personal guide to take me sightseeing, while Sande went to work. We flew from Brasilia to Sao Paulo. In Sao Paulo, the ladies of staff officers there took me for another pampering session, while Sande went about his work schedule. He got back to the hotel before I did. During that time, he received a phone call from my sister Nchimunya, to inform him that it was announced on the news that he had been retired as Air Force Commander. Immediately, he informed his Brazilian counterpart, and he downed tools.

I arrived at the hotel around 6 pm. I literally walked into a dark space, where Sande and his support staff were sitting. As soon as I walked in, I switched on the light and asked them why they were sitting in the dark." Sit down here, my wife," said Sande. I was excited about the shopping I had done, so I was very oblivious to the sombre faces everyone carried. I walked across with my hands barely supporting the heavy shopping bags and sat down. "I am no longer Commander of the Air Force," Sande informed me. "What! Are you serious?" I asked.

It then dawned on me why they were sitting in a gloomy, dark room; I needed no further explanation. I managed to say, "But we are still on duty. Can we at least finish the tour? It's just Rio-de-Janeiro remaining." Sande said: "No. I no longer have the mandate, my girl; we are heading back to Lusaka tomorrow."

Sande and Mutinta took a helicopter ride into Robben Island.

As the news sank in, I calmed down to listen to exactly what had happened. We called Zambia to speak to my sisters Chim and Nchimunya. Chim explained that at some point during the day, a driver came home to bring a letter for Sande. As per tradition, she pushed it under our bedroom door, which was locked. She said that another driver came through and picked up the official car from the house.

However, it was only during the evening news, that they learned that Sande was retired. Previously, there had been a regime change in Zambia, which ushered in a new President. It was therefore, expected that the new Commander-in-Chief would want to work with his own Commanders; however, the way it was done lacked decency.

We were left with no choice but to pack our bags in readiness for our trip back home. I looked at Sande, obviously wondering what might have been going through his mind. The only life he knew and loved was that of being a military officer, and he was retired while he was miles away from his office. I thought I would have to do some babysitting during the transition, but he told me that he slept very peacefully that night.

We flew back to London with a low-spirited team. The journey back from Sao Paulo to London seemed longer. Sande talked less but maintained his composure throughout. While flying, I picked up some courage and asked him if we could stop over in London on our way to Lusaka. Surprisingly, he agreed. I convinced him for us to spend a few days in London, so that we could let our hair down, before we could proceed home to face our new reality.

We took a week's break in East Croydon with our friends Iqbal and Sultana. When we finally got home, we were met by two officers who were assigned to meet us. It was a lukewarm welcome, contrary to the fun-fare that characterized our send-off. That reception cemented my thoughts that going forward, we were on our own.

We moved from the institutional house along Independence Avenue to our house in Makeni. While in Makeni, we tried to adapt to our new home. Apart from being on our own, the reality of where we were in our relationship became more pronounced.

While on the job, Sande's work got him too busy to the point where nothing and no one could come between him and his job. While I understood that as a military man, he pledged to serve country first, this reality tore us apart, as I expected him to prioritize family as much as country. The rift between us grew bigger as time went by, and our relationship suffered. Apart from the official assignments, we were not doing enough of what we used to do as a family together, in order to achieve couple growth.

Mwaji and Mashuta having some nibbles at Air House, Independence Avenue.

We were living with my baby sister Nachilala in the home. Nachilala is medium to tall, with an amber honey complexion; young, intelligent, and simply a high achiever. Without being told, she saw how the whole ordeal was wearing me down. "Sister, I need you to try and shift your focus to something within your control otherwise you will crash. Your whole happiness is wrapped around one person. However, your life is bigger than that.

Try to redefine your happiness around what is in your control, your children, your work, your educational improvement and your larger family." This advice did not sound like my fairy tale idea of marriage. Tough as the advice was, I decided to let my right foot off the accelerator pedal. It obviously meant that there was a shift in the relationship.

Before we could settle into retirement, we were subjected to investigations by the Task Force on corruption that was instituted by the second New Deal regime against the first New Deal regime, and Sande was not spared. I was to explain how I acquired plot No. 9 Jesmondine (Comfort Lodge), which I did. My husband also had accusations of abuse of office, which unfortunately led to a confiscation of his passport and an arrest.

This development threw the family off balance. Court became the new order. I was often confused, as I was in between court and prison. There was absolutely no time to attend to my businesses, as he had to feed three times a day, and the feeding times were four hours apart. From the glamour of being Air Force Commander's wife, I became the prisoner's wife. I stood by my husband's side through it all, with fortified support from my family. During my trips to and from prison, I asked myself how I would have survived this period, or answered the task force queries satisfactorily, if I took heed to the pressure to stop work and become a kept wife.

My children were too young to understand what was going on. Alas, some of their peers rubbed the news of the father's arrest in their faces. Mashuta was at Shengello Secondary School in, central Zambia. Some boys in his class repeatedly bullied him about this. He kept this news from us. We wondered why he carried a stressed face around until the sister Mwaji, brought it to our attention.

We verified this information with Tuttie, Gary's daughter, who was also at the same school.

Tuttie intimated that he was indeed being bullied by his friends, and as a result, he had only female friends and no male friends. We drove to Shengello and made it known to the school authorities. They suspended the boys for one week, and when they came back, they descended more on Mashuta with the help of other boys who identified with them.

Nachilala taking Mashuta out to Creamy Land for Ice-cream.

We had no choice but to pull Mashuta out of Shengello, to another school on recommendation from a counsellor we had engaged for him. We had him enrolled at Baobab College, which was a five-minute drive from our home. In no time, we noticed that he was doing well at Baobab. To this day, he affirms that contrary to Shengello School, Baobab gave him a wealth of friends, who did not thrive on name-dropping. Mashuta continued thriving at Baobab, and through his strong networks, he is today the Managing Director and Partner for Promo Basket, a Branding and Communications Company in Lusaka.

In 2009, Sande was convicted by the Magistrate's court, and sentenced to 7 years in prison. Through an appeal process, bail was secured for him, and we lived life one day at a time, not knowing what was coming our way. We struggled with this case for almost 12 years, starting from the Magistrate's Court, to the High Court, and finally to the Supreme Court.

At the end of the year 2022, while I was visiting my friend Chilufya in London, Mwaji called me to say that her father's appeal case was coming up for judgment that afternoon. I had some thought paralysis, mainly because I was so far away from my children. I prayed for a good outcome, and yes, it was granted. Justice was served. Sande was acquitted of all charges. I thanked the almighty God for this news. Although the family is currently apart, we all have peace of mind again.

Chapter 13
Conversations with my Mother

I came to realize that my parents' marriage was going through a rough patch in the early nineties. According to Mother, problems were always there, but she was counselled by her elders never to openly discuss her marital problems.

However, I was now married and old enough to see that the two were not growing together. In her heydays, my mother was a disciplinarian, and simply did not condone any unbecoming behaviour from anyone. She set herself for success in life and is a typical example of a smart and forward-thinking person.

This is what she typically expects of me, my siblings, and anyone who was privileged to be raised by her. Earlier in her trajectory, she acquired a number of properties in Livingstone, which are working for her to date.

On the other hand, my father was relatively less strict and easygoing. He was a good father to his children. He always thrived among us with his power of touch. He would take turns to lovingly pat our faces and stroke our hairs. Even when his expression of love messed up our hairstyles and makeup, it mattered less to him. This love he extended to all his kin, and everyone he encountered. He was by all standards the best brother, uncle, friend, and undoubtedly the best father, just by the way he seamlessly stitched us together as siblings. Sadly, my father failed the test of a good husband because he and my mother divorced in the 1990s.

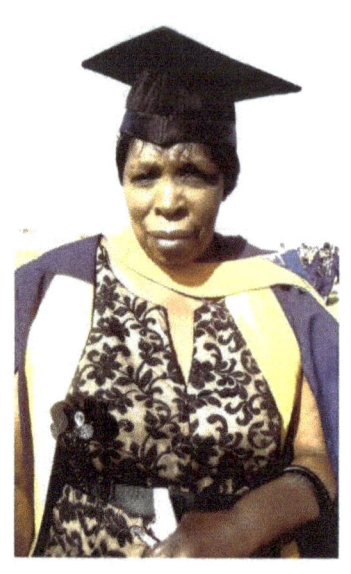

My mother Beatrice graduated with a Bachelor of Arts Degree in Adult Education from Zambia Open University.

According to my mother, she had reached the end of the road with him, and she asked for a divorce. My father visited me at my home on Independence Avenue. Being the eldest daughter of my mother, he asked me to try and convince her to change her mind about the divorce. I promised him that I would try.

Even if I promised my father that I would discuss the matter with her, I knew that he had broken his side of the vow, "to the exclusion of all others." He fathered children outside their marriage. Besides that, they had a myriad of other unresolved issues, and it was plain for us children to see. When it got out of hand, my mother would jokingly tell him that she was just waiting for her last-born child, Nachilala, to finish school, and she would be out of the marriage. I think for my father, it sounded like an empty threat, or maybe mere rhetoric, because he had heard it too many times.

My mother Beatrice on her 80th birthday at my home in Woodlands.

The assignment from my father meant having one of the most difficult conversations, a girl could ever have with her own mother. While I was expecting my first child, my mother came in from Livingstone, to orient me into motherhood. I procrastinated on having this discussion for a long time, while time was ticking. Maybe it is fair to say I was scared.

One day, while we were waiting for my baby's arrival, we sat on a reed mat outside on the lawn. I mustered some courage to discuss her pending divorce with my father. She spoke from her heart, as she laboured to make her point. She calmly said to me: "I will not have your father back in my life, and please respect my decision. You may not understand why I am doing this now, but I am praying that one day you will." She told me that something that was totally out of her control had occurred, and that it was irreversible. She assured me that no amount of arbitration would change her mind. Innocent lives were brought about in the process, and she had no power to change that. If she agreed to live with it, she was agreeing to live in misery and confusion for the rest of her life. She recalled how disappointed she felt at the breaking of this news, and that her decision to leave my father was a self-love move, which could only be understood by those who truly love themselves. She spoke with confidence, and she sounded like she had long prepared for the move.

As she warned, indeed, no amount of arbitration could change my mother's mind, and I did not have the muscle to change this either. She said she was deeply hurt and openly betrayed, which my poor father could not see. He did not know that his wife had long walked out of the marriage. The news of my father's retirement and planned departure for Nega Nega assisted her intended move.

Without an idea of her inarticulate plans, my father finally retired. He suggested that they go back to the land of Nega Nega in the Southern Province, where he had acquired a piece of land. My mother politely declined and told him that she was not going to Nega Nega with him because she had long left the marriage, which had irretrievably broken down by then.

My father moved to Nega Nega alone, and my mother took over the lease for the family house from the council. I had judged my mother very harshly. In my mind, I thought it was a huge embarrassment for the family to record a divorce. I did not know that divorce is actually a solution to a problem.

Following that discussion, I decided to respect her decision, as she implored me to. As for my father, he just had to swallow the bitter pill. It was a traditional marriage, and despite numerous deliberations with older relatives, my mother firmly stood her ground. They divorced.

Although Mother exhibited so much strength through the divorce, it was easy to tell that she was extremely hurt by the betrayal. She often lamented about her failed marriage and sang different choruses to reaffirm her decision. I listened to her many times, and it dawned on me that she was heartbroken; some counselling would have helped her.

Unfortunately, the issue of counselling was unheard of in her time. In Zambia, women are always encouraged to "shipikisha" (persevere) and not speak about their problems. She struggled in solitude in Livingstone for many years. My siblings and I managed to visit her whenever we could, but it was only for short periods. She, however, managed her time alone in a fashion of upward mobility. She bought the rented house on 22 Kombe Drive, when the Council announced the sale of council houses to sitting tenants. Before then, she had acquired a house in Dambwa North in Livingstone.

After her retirement, she went back to her practice of trading, but this time, she was selling second-hand clothes and anything that failed to sell in my shop. This business gave her a good return on investment, and in no time, she decided to extend her servant's quarter into a three-bedroom house, which she moved into in order to leave her main house on rent for some extra income.

My mother devised so many other ways to make money and keep herself busy. Apart from going to church every Sabbath, she enrolled herself at Zambia Open University in Lusaka to do her Bachelor's Degree, in Adult Education, through distance learning. She was 68 years old when she made this decision, but she refused to view her age as a limiting factor. Before then, she had been writing her GCE examinations in order to strengthen her certificate. She excelled in all her studies, but suffered a setback during her final year at university.

On one miserable Friday in August 2012, she was attacked in her home by unknown thieves who thought they left her dead. Around that time, my friend Mazuba Monze, popularly known as "Zu", and now Zambia's High Commissioner to South Africa, told me that she was planning to travel to Livingstone, and wanted to go and stay with my mother. Zu is medium height, fair-skinned, and forever bubbly. We met in Livingstone, where she lived with her husband Christopher. She was chosen as a matron of honour for a high-level wedding in Livingstone. I met her one day when she walked into my parents' home, to ask them if I could be one of the bridesmaids on that lineup. My parents agreed, and through the Zu-initiated lineup, I met Sandra. I advised Zu to just call my mother to inform her that she was going there. I knew that Zu didn't need me to ask on her behalf, because she and my mother always exchanged pleasantries.

Zu later called me to say she was concerned that Mother was not picking up her call. I was quick to advise her to try calling her in the evening after the Sabbath.

After Sabbath, Zu's call still went unanswered; at this point, I got concerned. I also made several attempts to reach my mother but without success. I called my siblings one after another to share my apprehension. Together, we decided to ask our cousins, Beene and Owen Nkombo, who lived in Livingstone, to go and check on her. They went there and somehow managed to get access to the house. They said the door to her house was wide open. They found her in the spare bedroom; the bedroom was in disarray, with beddings stained with blood. She was lying helplessly on the bed, bleeding profusely from her head, but they were able to tell that she still had a heartbeat. A distress call followed us to start off for Livingstone immediately. In the interim, they managed to get her to the Livingstone General Hospital. Choobe, Ben, Gary, and I immediately started off for Livingstone.

We stopped over in Monze to pick up my mother's elder sister, Aunty Leya. It was probably the longest trip I had ever taken to Livingstone. We tried to make conversation, mostly wondering what could have transpired, and what the bandits were looking for from an old woman like my mother. However, the silence in the car spoke more than we did. We were scared because we didn't know what we were going to find.

We went straight to the Livingstone General Hospital, where she was admitted. She could not talk. Intermittently, she could open her eyes, but she was in a non-responsive state. It was heartbreaking because she did not show any signs that she had recognized any one of us.

The nursing staff had shaved her whole head, which was swollen, to facilitate the suturing of the wounds, because the bandits hit her repeatedly in the head. We assessed her condition based on what we could see, and we immediately asked the doctor if we could fly her to Lusaka for more specialized treatment. Obviously, the doctor knew better than us, so he opposed the idea of flying.

Different from what we could see, he said my mother was in a critical state. Her level of consciousness was 5, and he warned that the mortuary state was 3. The pressurization on the aircraft would easily take her life away. He asked us to allow the hospital to raise her level of consciousness to at least 10, in order for us to move her using a road ambulance.

While waiting for her level of consciousness to rise, we decided to go to her home to check the crime scene. What we found there was jaw-dropping, and more boggling to the mind. There were blood stains all over the walls and the fridge, and things were strewn all over the place. We concluded that she must have put up a fight with the bandits. We got even more petrified when we saw a blood-stained hammer, with her white hair stuck to it. It was abandoned on the sitting room floor. The bandits must have used it to hammer her head. It is the reason why her hearing is impaired to this date. We picked up the hammer and surrendered it to the police as evidence.

That night was long and creepy. Choobe and I slept in Mother's bedroom, although we hardly slept because we were scared that the bandits would come back to finish us all. Gary and Ben took the other room, which looked tidier than Mother's room.

We requested an ambulance to take my mother to Lusaka, but Livingstone General Hospital said they had none. We, however, managed to arrange for a private ambulance through our networks. The next day, we were able to leave Livingstone for Lusaka around 03:00 after midnight. Aunt Leya took the seat in the ambulance, and we followed closely in another car.

We arrived in Lusaka around 10:00 hours. What a delight it was to find the Managing Director of the University Teaching Hospital (UTH) waiting for us in front of the hospital. My mother was immediately taken through a battery of tests, before she was wheeled to the intensive care unit (ICU). She was in the hospital for three weeks. This therefore, meant that our new base for that period was under a tree, at the UTH.

One afternoon, Velepi went to visit my mother in the ICU. She came back and told me that she found her humming some songs, something we all knew that she enjoyed. She encouraged me and my siblings to keep talking to her, even if she was not responding. She advised that she could still hear whatever was being said despite her condition. I talked to her each time I was in the ICU, mostly making positive affirmations about her recovery. I also sang some of her favourite tunes for days on end.

After two weeks of being on oxygen, she started regaining her consciousness, but was very incoherent. She was moved from ICU to a normal ward, where we were allowed to be by her bedside. We made a duty rota to be at her bedside, which worked very well. One evening, when Choobe and I were by her bedside, she repeatedly hallucinated about not knowing how to drive, and she ordered me to drive the car instead. She carried on hallucinating that evening. This made us suspect that the bandits might have been after her car, which we had gifted her on her 70th birthday.

The next morning, we decided to do away with the usual sponge bath that the hospital was giving her while in the ICU. We soaked her in a warm bath, and she immediately jacked up and started bathing herself excitedly. After the bath, she made it to sit in the wheelchair. We wheeled her outside the ward for some fresh air, much to the delight of the nursing staff. Everyone who visited her that morning wondered what trick we pulled for my mother to come around so quickly.

In her recovery process, she spoke about anything and everything, but never spoke of her experience with the bandits. The Neurologist, said there was a possibility that she would never have a recollection of what transpired. True to the Doctor's word, that part of her memory is still blocked to date.

The hospital staff called her the miracle mother; they put in their very best around her. Obviously, they were assisted by the mighty hand of God. After her discharge three weeks later, we agreed that she was never going to go back to Livingstone. The bandits are still on the loose to date. The police did not do anything about the case; they said they had no lead to the crime and were hoping that an interview with my mother could provide some information for them to work with. As the Neurologist advised, she has never had a recollection of what actually transpired, and to this day, we have never had any closure on her attack.

At that point, I feared her dreams of becoming a graduate were completely shattered. As a family, we asked Zambia Open University if they could give her an honorary degree, which they said they would consider, but my mother said she still wanted to give it a go. She was a long-distance scholar, and was only remaining with her dissertation to finish her degree.

She went ahead and did her dissertation under the supervision of one Owen Daka, (MHSRIP) and graduated at the age of 72.

It all seemed like a movie to see my mother clad in a graduation gown. Before then, I had bought her a new dress for her graduation and paid for her graduation ensemble. She took her place to graduate alongside many others, some fit to be her great-grandchildren. When the graduates were asked to toss their caps in the air, my poor mother missed it, because of her hearing problem, but clearly, she still stole the show. A newspaper reporter identified her and made an appointment to interview her. The next day, she took the front page of the Education Post newspaper, with the headline screaming, "When you give up, that is failing-Muyaba."

I was a very proud daughter to see my mother graduate. I congratulated her on her achievement, but it may be fair to say I was more challenged than proud. I began to reorganize my thinking in terms of furthering my education.

My mother was extremely unhappy with our decision to keep her from going back to Livingstone; she constantly pushed for me or one of my siblings to take her back. Sometimes, she would strongly agitate to go to her home, but we could not bring ourselves to do so, because we were scared to let her go back, especially that the bandits were still on the loose.

Sadly, with her constant agitation, she started showing signs of delusions again. We arranged professional counselling for her, and the counsellor took her right to the crime scene with the hope that there would be some recollection and subsequent closure, but all was in vain.

In her delirious state, my mother continued drumming in my ears, the idea of going back to school. In her own words, she repeatedly said to me that education is the best investment for the future.

"Mutinta, it's not enough for you to sit behind the counter and count money." I kept on hearing her say this in my mind. I was clearly challenged, but convinced beyond all reasonable doubt, that she was speaking sense, and that she was advocating for something achievable. Besides that, I had no excuse to give, because she had done it herself.

In her world of delusions, she dealt with big names such as Barack Obama and Queen Elizabeth. She once said to me that Barack Obama had sent 21 vehicles for her to start a car-hire business; she was asking if the cars could park at my yard in Makeni. She also believed that all the fancy perfumes and lotions we bought for her were sent for her by her best friend, Queen Elizabeth.

Challenging as my mother is, I still enjoy having diverse conversations with her, and she remains my driving force.

Chapter 14
The Challenge

I suddenly started having a deep reflection on my life. The business was going well, but my life felt empty, monotonous, and simply dreadful. My marriage was still severely challenged. I had so many gaps in my life; I was choking, and I needed an outlet. I no longer needed my mother's persuasion to go back to school.

On the other hand, I could also hear Nachilala's voice telling me to focus on my controllable sets. Going back to school was the only decent outlet, that could enable me to stay above the water. It was the one decision I had total control of, that could potentially close the many gaps.

During my time at ZNPF, I made sure I improved my grade 12 certificate. After the closure of Zambia Airways, I enrolled with the Chartered Institute of Marketing (CIM) in the UK. The course was being delivered by the Zambia Institute of Business College in Zambia (ZIBC). I failed to cope with school and the various chores I had to undertake, such as motherhood and business. I sacrificed the school with a plan to get back to it at a later stage.

One day, while sitting in my office at Comfort Lodge, I picked up the phone to call CIM in the UK. The pleasant voice on the other end confirmed that I had reached the Institute. I was informed that I was still a studying member with one course to pursue in order to attain a full Certificate in Marketing. She went on to say that if I did not finish that particular year, I was going to lose all the credits, and would have to start all over again. I panicked at hearing this pronouncement.

The lady went on to inform me that they had the Zambia Centre for Accountancy Studies (ZCAS) University, listed as a strategic partner for the course delivery. I immediately went to ZCAS and enrolled myself to continue with my studies.

While going back to school proved to be the best outlet for my struggles, it was one of the most humbling times of my life. This was because I found myself in class with kids of my children's age. I, however, told myself that this would not be a deterrent.

I finished the last course at the Certificate level and moved on to the diploma level. I struggled with one course, "Project Management," at the diploma level. I failed to clear it on my first attempt. It was on Digital Marketing, and in my mind, I thought it was as easy as it sounded, so I took a laissez-faire attitude towards it. Miserably so I had no choice but to repeat the course as I needed the credit in order to proceed to my Chartered Postgraduate Diploma level. I struggled with it and only managed to clear Project Management on my third attempt.

Towards the end of my Marketing course, my father fell ill, and was diagnosed with prostate cancer. He was admitted to the UTH for a procedure at the same time I was writing my final examinations. I remember very well how difficult this period was for me. I had to study and visit my father in between to deliver meals. I was in between home, ZCAS, and the hospital, often disoriented.

In the middle of all this, one day I got home only to find all my three-house help had been fired. I became more dis-oriented, but decided to turn a blind eye to this distraction.

With the entire house help fired, it simply meant that there was no one to cook food for the household, and for my father at the hospital because I was busy writing exams. My children were equally stressed, but I reminded them that they were old enough to do all the house chores, and even cook for themselves. For my ailing father's meals, I opted to pick takeaways from Comfort Lodge. I went ahead and wrote my exams despite all the confusion.

A check on the CIM portal a month later showed that I had cleared all my courses, and was invited to the UK for the graduation ceremony. I was extremely excited and looked forward to the trip. My father had also made a remarkable recovery by then.

It was the year 2013. I started gearing up for my graduation. I initially set out on a business trip to New York for re-stocking purposes. My itinerary was going to finally get me into the UK, to attend my graduation. I arrived in London two days before my graduation day. I made sure I bought my outfit out of New York.

Back in London, my friend Laura managed to secure, and collect my graduation kit. She sent me a picture of the gown, and I made sure my outfit matched it well. I wrapped up the business, air freighted the goods, and then jumped on the plane to London. I checked in at the Imperial Hotel, which was very close to Russell Square Train Station. A part of me was quite sad because I was all alone without family support.

Back in London, I was having a countdown to my graduation day, when a text message came through my phone. It was Gary. It read, "Mutikay, I am cruising at high altitude right now, coming to support you on your graduation, my girl." What a pleasant text message to read when I thought I was alone and so far away from home.

Gary had once intimated over a drink at Comfort Lodge that he might just come to witness my graduation, but I took it as a pep talk inspired by some alcoholic drinks. That was the best news I got on this trip. My whole thought process changed.

I graduated from Marketing school at Church House, London U.K in 2013.

Suddenly, I started planning our after-grad activities. I went down to the lobby of the Imperial Hotel to request another room for Gary. I messaged him back to say how delighted I was, and directed him to where I was staying. I told him to get off at Russell Square and crossover to the pub across the train station, where I would be waiting for him. I sat at the pub, waiting for him at his estimated time of arrival, and there he was. I was thrilled, and my excitement took me places.

We exchanged our hellos over a Gin and Tonic, and Stella Artois. We called for more rounds until we became completely new people. We remembered that the graduation was early the next day, so we had to stop and prepare for the big day. Hotel Imperial is a five-minute walk from the Russell Square train station. We walked to the hotel without realizing that something was amiss. When we got to the hotel, I needed to get the room keys from my handbag, only to discover that I was without it. Alas! I had left my handbag somewhere. The last place I had it was in the pub when paying the bar bill.

We rushed back to the empty pub, and my bag made a significant presence. It was hanging on the side of the chair where I sat. God was on my side. I did not lose a single thing. Thanks to the barman and his waiters. Gary noticed that I was going through an upheaval of emotions, and constantly teased me. Finally, I heard him say, "Mufana tekanya," meaning "Little one, take it easy."

The next day was the graduation day, which took place at Church House, Westminster, South West 1. Gary and I took a black taxi to the venue. It was a cold Saturday morning, and my dress looked like it was part of the graduation ensemble. I was not going to ruin the final look with a coat. I braved the cold.

Before I took my walk upstage, I met with other Zambians who were also graduating. They heard Gary and I converse in Tonga, so they reached out to us. We spoke to each other in Nyanja, and we took some graduation pictures together, too. My friend Laura also came to support me. After the graduation ceremony, the three of us checked into a Pub and Grill at Wood Green, where I was spoilt by the duo. Back home, my mother was very proud of me.

She repeatedly told me how happy I made her feel. The excitement was profound, and yes, I was proud of myself too.

I did not waste time after Marketing school. I immediately decided to enrol in a Master of Business Administration program with the University of Greenwich (UOG) UK. It was again to be delivered by the strategic partner ZCAS. I chose to study International Business. I used to go to work during the day and would attend class from 17:30 to 20:30 hours in the evening. I used my weekends for group work and assignments. This timetable inevitably saw me fall off the social grid, as I got extremely busy.

I, however, enjoyed every bit of my program, although I found it challenging at times. Apart from learning, I made new friends, most of whom were younger than me, but we could still have reasonable conversations. I took a liking to a girl called Elly Muzovu, and it looked like a mutual feeling, so we spent a lot of time together. I called her my walking stick because we did almost everything together.

I was particularly scared of the Financial Management and Accounting aspect of the course because I am very weak with numbers. I feared that if there was any failure in this program, it would only come from this course. A number of my classmates shared the same sentiments. We identified a guy called Imboela (Mhsrip), who we referred to as Bo Muluti, meaning teacher. He was good with the course and clearly a natural with numbers, and he gave us some extra lessons. It was a do-or-die case for me. I put everything I had into this course to the extent of dreaming numbers and formulae.

When the examination day arrived, I perused through the paper, and I knew before I started answering the questions that I had passed the examination. With the formulae engraved in my mind, I had absolutely no stress. When the results came out, I was awarded a merit in Financial Management and Accounting, and with that merit in my bag, I was sure I was going to conquer the MBA course.

I looked forward to going to school because home was lonely. With the children in university, the house was extremely quiet. The school became the perfect escape route for me. However, it brought about two things: a different kind of pressure, and because of staying up late to do assignments and study, my sleep completely escaped.

In the process, my marriage also got into more trouble. My children were attending university at Monash University in South Africa. I found time to go there to tell them that I was contemplating leaving home. I told them a little of what I thought was good for them to know. The two of them just said it was all up to me to do what I thought was best for me. That was not what I wanted to hear, but I had to remember that they could not relate to my problems because they spent more time in boarding school than at home.

I later went back to Lusaka. After a while, Mashuta decided to put his true feelings on paper about my intended move. He basically discouraged me from moving. He said I had lived and accepted that lifestyle all my married life, and nothing was likely to change, meaning I was expected to just accept things as they were. He decided to run the email by his uncle Gary before sending it to me. Gary advised him not to change anything and encouraged him to send it to me as it was. It made my heart bleed, that the two men who I loved so much, turned a blind eye to my predicament. They obviously had no idea about the magnitude of my problem.

Against all odds, I moved out of my matrimonial home, and rented a flat in Longacres in 2015. I was alone, and no one visited me there. But school was enough to fill the void. There was absolutely no contact between Sande and myself, until one day when my father called me to say he had been visited by Sande's friend Christopher. He intimated that Sande was asking for a meeting with us. I complied by driving to my father's farm in Nega Nega. After a whole day of deliberations, we were counselled, and we got back together.

Someone somewhere was not happy about the fact that Sande and I got back together. To add more stress to my already stressed life, a person called Chilufya Tayali put a story about me on his Facebook page. *(See Story on Page: 112)*

Almost all the social media platforms were buzzing with this story. It was a juicy story for people who did not know the truth, and it was definitely the kind of story that negative people thrive on. Sadly, most people believed it and circulated it many times.

They obviously were not privy to the fact that Sande did not have a passport to enable him to travel for a good ten years. It was confiscated at Lusaka International Airport, one afternoon after we arrived from South Africa, while he was under investigation. That was my reputation damaged. Something I worked so hard to build was ruined in a social media flash. I was angry for a moment, and all my defense instincts left me. God knows how I did not pop a blood vessel.

I had my suspicions about who was behind this write-up. I suspected that Chilufya was given this story by someone who was privy to my personal details and nuances. He made it his preoccupation to always take stock of what I owned. His collection of words and sensational writing, gave him away. I did not need to look far and wide. Upon reflection, I could not help but to think, that this person was assisting the forces who were trying to hound me out of the business world.

Sadly, I could not reverse anything. No amount of explaining would make the Zambian masses believe my side of the story, even if I was given a pedestal, and a megaphone to amplify my defense, I had already been judged.

The truth remains that I was never married in Turkey. In spite of this malicious writeup, I still love to go to Turkey, because it typically made me who I am today. It has always been, and remains my preferred destination, for business opportunities, and certainly not social pursuits. Without any doubt, I am well known and celebrated in Turkey, for my creditworthiness, and leaving stacks of cargo (pending collection) in shops, labelled Mutinda. (the closest approximation of my name that the Turks can pronounce).

Society is full of sick and broken people, living in a broken world, and wanting to transfer their brokenness to other people. Sande and I, however, visited my lawyer, Jason, with the idea of suing this Chilufya. However, Jason, who seemed to know better, that we would not get any compensation, advised us not to waste our time and money. Thus, we dropped the idea.

While all this was happening, I was still pursuing my master's program. Along the way, my father fell ill again. The cancer came back, and now with some vengeance. He was looking frail and it was easy to tell that he was no longer enjoying good health. I had to juggle life once more, this time taking care of business, myself, attending class, and taking care of my father. It became taxing because my father was in and out of the hospital. Often, he would ask whoever was at the bedside to massage his feet, which were always burning from the cancer that had obviously spread by this time.

One thing that made him feel better was to have his children around him. I remember one evening at the Lusaka Trust Hospital when the nurses signalled an end to the visiting hour; my father gently called the nurse and patted her on her shoulder in his usual affectionate way, and said to her, "Nurse, if you send away my children, I will die quickly." What followed was obvious: we were allowed a few more minutes to be with him. The hospital staff were clearly finding it difficult to manage this old man, who just wanted his children around him.

On the other hand, the general elections were approaching, and Gary was busy campaigning to defend his parliamentary seat in the Mazabuka central constituency. On Tuesday, 21st June 2016, he drove back to Lusaka to check on our father, who was being nursed from his home. I did not manage to see my father that Tuesday as I was busy with schoolwork. I had planned to see him the next day before anything else.

Gary arrived around 11:00 pm, just before midnight and went straight to check on him, after which he proceeded to sleep. It did not take long after this when my stepmother called him back for help. Having noticed that the situation had become dire, he called my sister Pitcairn, who works for the Lusaka Trust Hospital, and they agreed to meet there. He carried my father in his arms with the help of his friend Kenya Londe, the now Zambia's Deputy High Commissioner to Mozambique, placed him in the car, and drove him to the hospital. Upon arrival at the hospital, my father was hooked to oxygen to help him breathe.

My phone rang around 02:00 after midnight on Wednesday morning, it was Gary, and he said, "Mutikay, I want you to drive slowly to the hospital. Father is not looking good." I got into my car and drove through the darkened night, consumed by strange imaginations of what the hospital situation was like.

I found my father on oxygen and non-responsive. I was devastated. Gary also called the rest of my siblings who were staying in Lusaka and one by one, they all came to the hospital. We hung around the hospital until dawn, and then Gary asked me to take my stepmother home so that she could catch some rest. Alas! At around 10:00 hours in the morning, Gary called again to say our father was gone.

I felt numb and could not think. I had a blinded sense of how to engage the gears on my Toyota Hilux, so I asked Charles, who was doing some maintenance work around the house, to drive me back to the hospital.

My father was still on his dying bed. I got there in time to give him the last hug, and see his body being repatriated to Ideal Funeral Home. This was the most difficult time of my life. Gary and I drove behind the hearse, which was carrying our father's body, to Ideal Funeral Home. I thought I was of age, but seriously, you are never old enough to lose a parent.

My MBA graduation at the University of Greenwich UK- 2016.

We immediately started preparing to move the funeral to our family farm in Nega Nega. We moved the body the very next day in preparation for burial on Friday. My father was a people person, and the crowd that appeared in Nega Nega was enough testimony to that. All roads led to Nega Nega, and minibus operators abandoned their usual routes, to cash in on the Nkombo funeral. The numbers were too big to be accommodated in the local church, so we held the church service outside our family home in a marquee, and later put him to rest at the family burial site.

By this time, I had completed my MBA program. My graduation was scheduled for the very next month after my father's funeral. As I prepared to travel, I thought to myself how happy he would have been if he had lived to see me graduate. I went to England with my new friend Elly. This time, my family support was my daughter, Mwaji, who was also doing her MSc in International Business, at the University of Coventry in England.

I took a majestic walk as my name was called out to receive my degree. The excitement added a spring to my stride as I graduated with distinction. I was very pleased with myself. Mwaji was very happy and proud of me too, but failed to pronounce the pressure that I left her under. She was also towards the end of her stint at Coventry University, literally doing her dissertation. My mother was even happier. The words that stuck with me in her congratulatory message were, "I told you that you could do it, Mutinta. When you give up, that is failing."

A few months later, in April 2017, Sande had just gotten his passport back from the system. It was an exciting moment for the family because we could travel together again.

We left Lusaka for South Africa to attend Mashuta's graduation ceremony at Monash University, and then we proceeded to England to attend Mwaji's graduation at Coventry University. The two alluded to the fact that I left them under pressure when I graduated with distinction.

After all was said and done, there was success everywhere, and we were all happy graduates.

Zambia Reports
14 Dec 2015 ·

EX-ZAF Commander Shattered; Wife Married in Turkey

By Chilufya Tayali

Former ZAF commander Sande Kayumba, owner of Comfort Lodge along Great East Road in Lusaka, had a major shock when he followed his wife Mutinta Nkombo (Mazabuka MP Gary Nkombo's sister) to Turkey only to find that she has allegedly been married to another man there for years.

Mutinta regularly leaves her matrimonial home in Lusaka and usually travels to Turkey and "Italy" where she regularly buys fashion stuff for her boutiques in Lusaka.

It remains unknown what picked Kayumba's suspicion when he decided to check on his wife's whereabout abroad and followed her to Turkey.

He allegedly quickly learnt that the Hotel she posts as being her residence during her shopping for Boutiques expressed ignorance of her presence there.

With his military skills of "search and rescue", Kayumba established that the wife lived at her "second matrimonial" home. Kayumba has been jailed for corruption but he is out on bail pending appeal.

He is said to have put all his properties in her name. Kayumba ditched his first wife for her when she was a Zambia Airways Air Hostess.

Kayumba is now said to have lapsed into a serious case of depression. He has been married to Mutinta for the last 25 years. He is completely shattered.

Chapter 15
The Castle

When Sande's tour of duty ended, we shifted from the institutional house to our own home in Makeni. A part of me was sad, and the other part was excited because I thought that with the demanding job behind us, we would fall back on our old rituals: watching our favourite soap, Isidingo, and playing squash together. However, this did not happen because by this time, we were perfectly estranged.

At the time we were moving into the Makeni house, I thought that the house was big enough, as it was an existing four-bedroomed house, with a lot of space especially in the main lounge and the TV room. Sande likes big houses, so he embarked on an expansion exercise for the house. He extended it by another six bedrooms, three of which were upstairs.

We therefore, ended up with a ten-bedroom house with three living rooms, one office, a bar, and one humongous kitchen. He called it the Castle. By this time, we had weaned off all our dependants, as they were either married or living on their own. We remained the two of us, only to be swallowed by the castle.

My kids came back home from university, and our lives continued on this trajectory. Even the presence of the children did not help the situation. I started looking for options.

Mwaji and Mashuta were fortunate to immediately get employed by Africa Management Services Company and Specialty Emergency Services (SES) Zambia, respectively. It was such a pleasant coincidence that they started work on the same day.

One evening, after getting home from work, Mwaji came and lay with me in my bed. She said she had some good news for me. She told me that Musonda Mbalazi, her long-time friend, had proposed marriage to her. This was very good news for the family, although it gave me a chill. I froze and went mute for some time, reflecting on my own marriage, which was failing.

Musonda is my nephew Ubinga's friend. Ubinga is Gary and Katendi's first child. We knew Musonda as a mere friend to Ubinga, and Mwaji. Ubinga later told me that the moment he introduced Musonda to his sister, Mwaji, he knew without doubt that the two would get married one day.

Musonda lived in the neighbourhood, literally ten minutes away from us. After some time, I settled down with the news and found time to tell Sande about it. I prayed for a happy union for my daughter and her husband-to-be. As time went by, my anxieties were put to rest, when I came to know that the two were actually best friends. They did a lot of things together, including going to church.

Our home was suddenly blessed with so much joy and laughter, when one afternoon, a team of happy people from Musonda's family came to officially ask for my daughter, Mwaji's hand in marriage. The marriage negotiations went very well, and everything was agreed by both parties. This interaction almost became a party as we had drinks and snacks after the talks. Mwaji was given a surprise engagement party by Musonda the same evening after the talks.

The atmosphere in the home changed. Suddenly, there was a lot of hype about the bridal shower and wedding preparations. I took it upon myself to give my daughter a memorable send-off. I went on to tender the gardens at home in preparation for the bridal shower. It was a good distraction.

My cousin Catherine, was by this time, running the 3Sixty Convention Centre, (a conference and wedding venue) with her husband, David. I hired her to manage the whole bridal shower event at my home. She pitched a 400-capacity marquee in front of the Castle. She did the all-white decoration and provided the outside catering for the event.

I proudly hosted Mwaji's bridal shower at our home in Makeni. Immediately after the bridal shower, we went into preparations for the wedding, which started with a very beautiful marriage ceremony at the Lusaka Baptist Church in Longacres, followed by a reception at the Taj Pamodzi Hotel lawns in Lusaka. Musonda's mother, Patricia Milimo, and I worked well together to ensure we created good memories for our children.

Soon after Mwaji got married, Mashuta also made his announcement that he was moving out of the castle. He had found a house for rent, which he was going to be sharing with a friend. They both left our Makeni home. As the children departed, we were left on our own once again, and the Castle completely swallowed us.

My daughter Mwaji married her best friend Musonda at the Taj Pamodzi Hotel in 2018.

Chapter 16
Prescriptions of Life

Apart from the day, I came to life, I was first admitted to the hospital when I was due to deliver my daughter, Mwaji. Prior to that, I had never known what sleeping in a hospital bed was like. I think it is fair to say that for the longest time, I lived a healthy life. Unfortunately, it did not stay like that.

Just before we left the ZAF institutional house, I started having feelings of dizziness, headache, heart palpitations, and general anxiety. It was not a feeling one could ignore. I checked in at the Pearl of Health Clinic to consult with Dr Phiri, a cardiologist and retired General in the Zambia Army. He took me through a thorough investigation, and discovered that my blood pressure was high. He gave me medication and quickly referred me to Dr Gracia, a kidney specialist, without telling me what the actual problem was.

Dr. Gracia's clinic was my preferred clinic for my whole family to attend when I got married. She came highly recommended by a mutual friend, so I had the whole family registered there. In an unfortunate turn of events, Sande instructed me to transfer the family membership from Dr Gracia's clinic to an alternative facility. However, after an extensive search, I was unable to find a suitable replacement for a long time. Consequently, the family sought medical attention at the military hospital located on Independence Avenue in Maina Soko Hospital. I did not have a reason to give Dr Gracia for deserting her clinic, so I simply walked away.

As fate had it, Dr Phiri's findings led me back to Dr Gracia. She was professional and gracious as always. She did not even ask me why I had left in the first place. After reading the referral letter, she carried out her independent investigations, and informed me that my kidney had a problem. She however, said that the stage at which the problem was detected was early and that if I followed her instructions, I could live like that for a long time to come.

I was devastated by her pronouncement, but she counselled me not to worry too much, as worry would only make things worse. She put me on blood pressure medication, which would tightly control my blood pressure in order to protect my kidney.

Along the way, she advised that I do my HIV test, which if positive, would have to change the whole treatment plan. There was still a lot of stigma surrounding HIV then. I procrastinated around this decision, but she did not push me at all. This was in 2008, and to this day, I make routine quarterly visits to Dr Gracia, and that part of my life is still going well.

On the other hand, the anxiety earlier presented brought about insomnia; therefore, she gave me medicine for that. I was on and off pills for a long time, and that in itself was depressing. I knew when I did not sleep well because the following day, I would be lethargic and highly irritable. I resorted to doing a lot of exercises, all in search of my feel-good hormones. I also embraced the sauna for relaxation. A book I read entitled "Less Stress" by Dr Julian Melgosa, guided one to heat up the body in the sauna for 15-minute intervals, and then shock it with a cold shower or a dip in the swimming pool. The action was to be repeated 3 times, without exceeding a total session of 45 minutes. That became my home therapy, and each time I did it, it relaxed me to sleep.

In trying to manage my stress and save my marriage, I decided to engage a psycho-social counsellor, Mr Kamau, where Sande and I attended some reconciliatory sessions to try and bring us back together. This process failed lamentably.

When this failed, I looked for another Psychologist, this time for my own personal healing. I discovered Dr Davies and Sande opted to join me in these sessions again. Unfortunately, this one failed too. The Psychologist advised us that counselling does not just require presence, but full participation from both parties, otherwise, we were wasting our time. Sometimes, we were given a couple of assignments to do at home, and we did not do them. She said that as long as the assignments were not done, there was no way of carrying on, and she had no way of helping us.

We left Dr Davies without resolving our issues. I then decided to go to a wellness centre on the riverside in Kafue for a retreat. Sande decided to come with me again. The Riverside counselled us mainly on biblical teachings about marriage, nutrition, and natural methods of healing for my insomnia. We stayed there for a week, which brought us back to peace for some time.

After the stint at Riverside, the insomnia was still there. The insomnia, however, brought about other health-related problems. Everything I was going through manifested on my face. My face broke out with severe acne, which changed my whole outlook. I could not manage to leave my house without a thick layer of makeup, although even makeup failed to mask the anxiety on my face. I could no longer walk with my head up, and my confidence left me.

I visited my local pharmacist, Mr. Tembo, who tried all sorts of creams without any success. Later on, I went to see a skin doctor, Dr Ernest, who prescribed some oral medicine and a cream for applying on the face. He assured me that at the end of that therapy, my skin would be like that of a baby.

I was excited, and looked forward to starting the therapy. I sent the prescription with my driver to Mr. Tembo. He decided to call me because he had concerns about the medication."Mrs. Kayumba, I need to see you. I will not give this medicine to the driver. The medicine prescribed for you has very bad side effects."

I braved the trip to the pharmacy to try and convince him to give me the medicine. He said to me, "Madam, we have tried all sorts of creams on your face. Sometimes, the way you feel inside manifests on your physical being. I will not give you this medicine, because you are still young, and the side effects are harsh. You may still want to have more children in the future." I concluded that the medicine was lethal. With that information in my hands, I stopped pursuing him. After that, he prescribed many other creams, which still did not work. I then decided to look elsewhere for treatment.

I went to Pretoria, South Africa, where I had an appointment to see a Psychiatrist, Dr Laurian, at Louis Pasteur Hospital. I arranged to stay with my friend Dr Connie Osborne, whom I met through Lanette. Lanette and I had planned a business trip to Beijing, and she arranged for us to stay with Connie. At the last minute, Lanette suffered a setback and could not travel. Connie was still gracious enough to take me to her home. Connie is a short and fair lady with a beautiful soul. She is a few years older than me but really fun to have around. She calls me Tinti. When I arrived at the train station in Pretoria, I found her waiting for me.

The first thing she noticed was my troubled face. She sympathized with my situation, which she attributed to insomnia. At that time, she had no idea I had marital difficulties, as I was still in the business of masking my emotions. She gave me a car to get around while in Pretoria. I went to the hospital the next day and saw Dr Laurian. He heard my story and advised that before he could give me medicines, he wanted to teach me breathing exercises for relaxation. I continued seeing him for two weeks, and then it was time to return to Lusaka. At the end of two weeks, my sleep had not improved, so he also administered pills.

After my first session with Dr Laurian, I walked around the hospital in search of a laboratory. I had resolved within myself, that it was inevitable for me to do the HIV test, given the breakout on my face, and Dr Gracia's advice. I found a Lancet laboratory and walked in with a drawn face, to request the HIV test. The nurse asked if I had been counselled, to which I answered no. I was offered counselling, but I refused. She drew the blood from me and told me that the results would only be known after three days. "What a lot of waiting," I said to myself. At that point, I wished I had accepted the counselling.

I drove back to Connie's house. In the evening, we were having a chat in her bedroom, when I noticed stacks of HIV self-testing kits. My heart skipped a beat. "I could have just asked her to test me from home and gotten the results instantly."

But then, I did not even have the courage to discuss it with her, because of the stigma around HIV. All she knew was that I was just seeing Dr Laurian for my insomnia. The temptation to just get one kit and test myself was high, but I restrained myself for fear of causing a false alarm. The three days seemed prolonged, and the fact that I kept it away from Connie, meant that I had no sounding board.

I tried to pass the time the way I know best, shopping, but nothing was good enough to settle my anxious mind.

On the third day, I took a drive to the hospital; driving very slowly, but constantly slamming the brakes. I entered the Lancet laboratory, and while gnashing my teeth, I presented my receipt to the gentleman who was manning the office. He immediately printed out my results, put them in a plastic sleeve, and passed them on to me.

I opened the sleeve, got the report out and looked everywhere for a negative. I was consumed by anxiety, and therefore, convinced myself that the results were inconclusive. I reached out to the nurse who took my blood earlier for help. She got the paper with the results and said, "You are non-reactive, which means you are negative."

That was all I wanted to hear. I strolled quietly into one of the common rest areas, knelt down, and started singing praises to God, and after that, I said a prayer. I was still troubled about my facial appearance, although the result gave me a layer of confidence.

I left the hospital very excited. I did not know where I was going, but the car was moving. Suddenly the phone rang, it was Connie and it was a Friday afternoon, and she had finished work for the day.

"Tinti, please come and join me for lunch at the Village restaurant," she said. I turned the car around to find my way to the restaurant. I was suddenly ready to talk about the test, and I could not wait to break the news to Connie.

Finally, when I got there, I quickly broke the news. Dr C, as I often call her, "I did my HIV test three days ago, and here is my result." Truthfully speaking, I needed her to re-confirm the meaning of the non-reactive narration, which she did. In response, she said, "Oh! Tinti, that is so nice, but why didn't you just ask me to do the test for you at home? I have a lot of test kits." I smiled and silently responded to her, "The reason why I have been looking so pensive from the time I came." We had our lunch and had some Sherry too.

Finally, I had a result for Gracia, and that worry was erased from my mind, but the insomnia was still there. Dr Laurian referred me to a sleep doctor at Morning Side Clinic, Dr Ross. He outlined to me all the possible causes of insomnia, stress, anxiety, trauma, enlarged tonsils, et cetera. On top of the medicines I was given by Dr Laurian, he introduced me to some sleep hygiene, which included sleeping at the same time every day. He extended my bedtime to midnight so that I could get more tired. He advised against watching television in bed. He also advised that if I stayed in bed for 20 minutes without sleeping, then I had to get up and do something else. Therefore, I had to find a hobby. I started knitting.

Apart from this regime, I had to keep a sleep diary to note how many hours I slept every night, and how I felt in the morning, whether rested or lethargic. He noticed my troubled face, and then he referred me to Dr Marcia, a skin doctor within Morning Side. She also did her independent investigations, and at the end of it, I had a whole buffet of medicines. She gave me both oral and some medicines to apply on the face.

When I got back home, I started taking the medicines, and after some time, I realized that the sleep had now completely escaped. Among the medicines she gave me was a tablet called Dapsone. My instinct led me to Google to find out its side effects, and insomnia was one of them. I called Dr Marcia to tell her about the Dapsone. She confirmed that Dapsone causes insomnia in certain people, and she advised me to stop taking it.

At some point, after I got back home, I had to go to India to escort a family member for treatment. We landed in Cochin in the Kerala state of India. I also took a chance to do a full medical check-up. Everything went well, apart from the fact that I was told that I had inflamed tonsils.

After 3 weeks, we left India and stopped over in South Africa, Johannesburg, where my sister Nachilala was living. My idea was now to seek a homoeopathy intervention for my sleep. I saw Dr Yu, who suggested acupuncture. It was to be done over a long period of time. So, it made sense that we left Johannesburg for Zambia, so that my patient would recuperate from home comfortably.

After one week, I went back to Johannesburg to do the acupuncture therapy. Painful needles were inserted into my body on alternate days for one month. Sometimes, I got relief, but often times not. Then, Dr Yu advised me to see a psychologist on the days when I was not having needles. He referred me to a Dr Mindy.

In our discussions, Mindy picked up that I was severely depressed. Her plan was to approach my illness using a wide variety of tools and resources. She recommended Cognitive Behavioral Therapy (CBT). She told me that CBT is a practical type of talking therapy, and problem-solving technique, that focuses on the relationship between thoughts, feelings, beliefs, and behaviours. Her idea was to break the cycle of negative thoughts, and the things that were affecting me at the time. She, however, advised that it was impossible for healing to happen in a toxic environment. I attended the therapy for another two weeks. After the counselling and acupuncture sessions were over, I returned to Zambia to face my reality.

In 2017, it became necessary for my inflamed tonsils to be removed. Dr. Ross had also intimated that my tonsils could have possibly caused insomnia, because they were almost closing my airway. We jetted back to Cochin. Pre-surgery tests were done on me, to prepare for my tonsils to be removed. It was my hope that the removal of the tonsils would finally resolve my insomnia.

The surgery went very well, but it was a painful experience. What was more painful was being made to eat toasted bread, and Chicken Tikka a day after the surgery. We returned home two weeks later, but my sleep still did not improve.

Chapter 17
Back to Livingstone

My mother started showing signs of being unwell again in 2015. Apart from the delusions, she was always pushing to go back to her home in Livingstone, but we did not grant her request. According to her, she was tired of living in our homes. We tried to take her to the hospital but failed to convince her that she was unwell. We later realized that refusing to go to the hospital was part of her protest, so we arranged for a doctor to visit her at Nchimunya's home, where she was living.

Dr Kumar was gracious enough to pay her a home visit. The doctor's diagnosis was that my mother was showing signs of dementia. He started by counselling us and informed us that there was no cure for dementia, but only some medication that could help suppress her illusions and anxieties. We started giving my mother the medication, which we had to disguise in food or drink, as she would not willingly take the medicines.

He advised us to brace ourselves for tougher times, and take her illness within our strides, as often dementia only gets worse, and leaves caregivers more drained than the patient. He also advised that sometimes dementia patients do well in an environment which they are more familiar with. We managed to keep her for about three years with this method of medicating. Unfortunately, the agitation did not stop, but we had learned the skills of how to manage her illness.

At some point in 2018, the agitation intensified, so my siblings and I decided to try and take her to her home in Livingstone, which was a familiar space for her. At this point, I started toying with the idea of being the one to take her back to her home. I was going to be with her for as long as I was able to. I began to renovate my mother's house in order to make it comfortable for us.

After Mwaji's wedding in December of 2018, my siblings and I took off for Livingstone in a convoy. We all planned to have Christmas and New Year with her, before the rest of my siblings would head back to Lusaka. We wanted to see if she would do better there compared to Lusaka.

The joy my mother exhibited when we arrived in Livingstone was remarkable. She walked around her house. I had renovated and extended it, making her bedroom and mine self-contained. I had it decorated, air-conditioned and done some landscaping. It was a delight to look at. In my mother's world, her "friend" Queen Elizabeth had done all the renovations for her.

This was the first time my mother was back in Livingstone after her attack in 2012, exactly six years later. As a result, we were all anxious as to what her reaction would be. We unanimously agreed that we needed prayers. We arranged for her close friends and churchmates to come home for dinner the day after we arrived. She was received well by everybody. The elders at her church came and worshipped with us and blessed her home.

We did the Victoria Falls tours; we went on the famous Toanga Boat Cruise, and drove around to show our children how we lived life in Livingstone then. After all the festivities were behind us, everyone went back to Lusaka, and I stayed behind in Livingstone.

I could tell that my mother was very happy to be back home, just by the way she gave instructions to the workers. She was in charge of her domain; the teacher in her came out, and often, our instructions to the workers clashed. I often had to pull back and remember that it was her house.

The veranda of her house was our favourite chill spot, so I placed two reclining chairs there for us. We sang songs together, and danced to her favourite song, Dadoo Ron Ron, by Shaun Cassidy, and many others. We also played a board game called Nsolo (a Zambian version of Mancala), which helped to jack up her memory and observation skills. On alternate days, she watched me grow my love for gardening, as I transformed the quicksand that surrounded her house into a plush garden.

During the four months that I stayed with my mother, I could tell that leaving her alone would be irresponsible, because she could no longer do anything for herself. Sometimes, she would wake up in the middle of the night, get dressed, and come to knock on my bedroom door, to ask me to open the door for her. In her world, there were friends outside waiting to take her to watch a movie.

On other days, she accused me of stealing her Oil of Olay, which was sent to her by Queen Elizabeth. Some days, she woke up in the mood to cook. She loved cooking so much, but whatever food she attempted to cook got burnt, because at some point, she would forget that she was cooking. One night, she got up and started cooking, and she forgot that she had left a pot on a hot plate. I was choking, and that woke me up from my sleep, only to find the house was filled with smoke.

After that episode, I made it my routine to switch off the stove power from the mains at night. I suggested to my siblings that at any given time, one of us needed to be with my mother in Livingstone, although it proved to be impossible. I could not leave my mother as long as there was no one to relieve me. My female siblings were all in formal employment, so they could not fit into the shifts. At some point, I desperately needed to travel to Lusaka, so I left her with a good set of workers, but it turned out to be one of my most difficult moments. My heart was always in Livingstone. As a result, I found myself driving back and forth to check on her.

In Livingstone, my sleep diary showed that I had achieved a good four hours of sleep, without any medical intervention. The moment I got back to Lusaka, the insomnia came back. I remembered the words of Dr Mindy, the Psychologist, "Mutinta, you will never heal as long as you are in a toxic environment." I had no choice but to go back to the Doctor, who administered pills again.

Chapter 18
Stepping into the Unknown

I woke up one day and started reflecting on my life again. As I lay in bed, my mind started to wander. All efforts to bring it back to the now, failed, as it was going back to my situation-ship. I felt like I was walking on quicksand, because I kept going down. Above all, I was lonely and often trapped in a thought paralysis. I thought I was strong; but clearly, I got tired of being strong, so I crashed. Nachilala had counselled me to avoid a crash landing, but I guess it was too late.

I started entertaining the idea of leaving my home. I prayed to God for guidance, and he led me to Ecclesiastes 3:5-6: a time to scatter stones and a time to gather them; a time to embrace and a time to refrain from embracing; a time to search and a time to give up; a time to keep and a time to throw away. Apart from God's word, I was counselled that I needed to pamper myself with some self-love, in order to be able to take such a giant step. I felt duty-bound to love myself.

In spite of the counselling I had received earlier, I told myself to try to make our relationship work one more time. Before I left, I started suggesting to Sande that we move out of the "Castle" to our Woodlands house, which was smaller, but more intimate. This was with the hope that a smaller space would re-align us.

I started renovating the house in Woodlands. Periodically, Sande would pass through there to see what was happening, and he said that I was doing a good job. I made sure I replicated all the facilities we had at the "Castle", albeit in a small way. I did not want him to say he was missing anything away from there. I made sure there was a home office, sauna, and swimming pool, as we both liked the sauna-swim therapy.

Then, one day, he asked me what we were going to do with the Castle if we moved. That made me believe that he was contemplating the move. I said either turn it into a lodge, or better still, sell it and enjoy our money, after all the children were grown up and gone. I got it all wrong.

It was during the COVID-19 pandemic. Families were encouraged to keep to themselves, so I did not see my family members for a long time. Back home, I became even more lonely. We were perfectly estranged, and our minds were far apart, making mutual growth impossible. Our paths failed to align after close to three decades. Often, I cried to sleep at the thought of taking this route that is seldom used. Petrifying as the thought was, I counselled myself to go through the hurt in order to grow through it. Leaving became the only alternative as it would provide an opportunity for me to heal. I also believed that my departure would give both of us clarity on the value that we placed on each other.

I packed up my clothes and told him that I was going to live in Woodlands. I had just recovered from a COVID attack, and I left the Castle to an empty house in Woodlands. I did not even have any house help. There was nothing to do anyway, as the emptiness of the house gazed at me every day. I left the Castle, all corners filled with decor, to a house whose corners were begging.

Slowly but surely, I started filling up the corners. I dressed the floors with carpets one room at a time, and things began to shape up. I looked outside, and the surroundings were unkempt. Tall grass surrounded the house, and it was normal to find at least one snake in a week. With very little knowledge and experience on gardening, I decided to take up the challenge as part of my healing therapy. I cleared the whole surrounding, planted grass and flowers, and paved the driveway. Before I realized it, I had created at sanctuary.

About six months after my departure from the Castle, Katendi went to Livingstone for work. She found time to go and check on my mother. She called me to say that she found her sleeping at an hour when she should have been awake. She said she was looking unhappy and disoriented. She put her on a WhatsApp video call for us to see how she looked. We agreed with her assessment that it was better to bring my mother back to Lusaka.

A few days later, Gary and my young sister Cholwe left Lusaka at 04:00 after midnight to go and fetch her from Livingstone. They had to come up with a convincing story as to why they were picking her up. They told her that they were picking her up to spend Christmas with us in Lusaka, and she obliged. They arrived back in Lusaka at 21:00 hours the same day with her. That was the Christmas period of the year 2020.

On the eve of Christmas, we all drove to Gary's home in Shimabala, where we camped to wait for Christmas day. We were all happy, and my mother looked happy too, at least for that moment.

Going forward, we resolved that after that, she was going to live with me in Woodlands. It did not take very long after the festive period, before she started agitating to go back to her home in Livingstone.

I am still living with my mother today, but day after day, month after month, she wakes up and packs her clothes, because she would like to go back to her home. In the morning, her bags are packed and positioned on the veranda, waiting for Gary or Ben to come and take her back to Livingstone. When she gives up in the evening, we have to move things back into her bedroom.

There are times when we engage in some challenging conversations, and I get surprised as to how she still articulates issues. I guess it's the twists and turns of dementia. Her Doctor advised us that the back and forth was normal behaviour for a dementia patient.

My mother still plays Nsolo, especially with her grandchildren and the house help. One thing for sure is that she has mastered this game, as beating her is still a challenge. All that said, my mother's illness has had a positive effect on me as a person. I am naturally always in a hurry, but I have had to slow down around my mother. I always strive to create peace, just by allowing her to do what she wants, unless it poses a danger to her.

On the day her "friend" Queen Elizabeth died, I took time to tell her the sad news. When I got back home in the evening, she asked if we were going to sleep at the funeral, following our Zambian tradition. That is dementia at its best.

To those affected by dementia either directly or indirectly, I give you my embrace. Dementia is often misunderstood and stigmatized due to cultural and societal factors. The best you can do for a patient is; to create a safe environment, accept their emotions, use simple language, be patient and offer choices and establish routines to provide structure and familiarity. To the care giver; be understanding, empathetic, educate yourself about dementia and do not forget to take care of yourself.

When one door closes, God opens another door. In my case, my departure from the Castle gave me an opportunity to take care of my ailing mother, twenty-four-seven.

Chapter 19
Grand Central

My home in Woodlands is very centrally located. My family are in and out of my home, because of its close proximity to everything. Someone drops in to say hello to my mother literally every day. Because of this, there is usually a big pyramid of Nshima and Chibwantu for whoever passes through.

So many nicknames were floated for my house, such as Kings Cross, Grand Central Station, and GO Residence. Those who called it Grand Central Station won. My nephew Mwitelela (my late sister Odiyee's son) even bought a clock for my veranda engraved "Grand Central."

Everyone loves it here, and those who have experienced Grand Central Station in New York, know exactly what it is like; all trains meet at Grand Central station. In my case, my kin meet at my home mostly to check on my mother. Sometimes, everyone shows up at the same time, and it gets groovy.

I have my lonely moments at Grand Central, but the frequent visits from my family have kept me going. I had to, therefore, come up with some activities to fill the void. I started gardening as a hobby, and realized that it required a lot of consistency. Apart from that, there was a lot to learn in the garden. I used the knowledge I acquired from friends to develop my garden. I also thought of starting to learn how to play golf.

I was in Johannesburg with my friend Sarah Ng'andu. I met Sarah when I joined Zambia Airways. Sarah is medium to tall in height, brown in complexion, and admirable in many ways.

She is the one friend with whom we share the same clothes size all around. We also seem to have the same taste in clothes by the things we buy independently of each other. We were in the Pro-shop in Wood Mead in South Africa in the year 2020. We agreed to start learning Golf. While in the Pro Shop, we paid for our Golf kits and attire.

When we got back to Lusaka, we enrolled for Golf lessons at the Bonanza Golf Club. After six weeks of theory and practical lessons, we were tested, given our certificates, and were ready to go on the course. The hours spent gardening and on the golf course assisted greatly in filling the void.

My home has continued to be the rendezvous for my family. The Veranda is my favourite joint. A lot of diverse issues are discussed here by my friends and family, including politics. Towards the run-up to the 2021 general elections, my place became a hive of activity, and this one somehow kept me going too.

Zambia went through general elections to usher in the 7th Republican President. Cholwe and I went into Mazabuka to assist Gary with campaigns. After the elections, my family gathered at Grand Central to wait for the results, which were coming in a little at a time. It took three days before the final results were announced.

On the day the final results were going to be announced, we sat in my veranda until very late to hear the pronouncement. The pronouncement was exactly the way we wanted to hear it. This election ushered the UPND government into office under the Leadership of President Hakainde Hichilema. The television became irrelevant after the pronouncement. We did high fives, toasted, danced, and repeatedly sang the UPND choruses. Before we realized, it was dawn.

A few days later, National Heroes Stadium was filled to capacity, for the Presidential inauguration ceremony. My boutique also received some limelight. Everyone wanted to wear something new for the inauguration ceremony. We cashed in. There was jubilation as people paraded the streets to express their happiness. My siblings and I joined in the celebrations.

I started learning how to play golf at Bonanza Ciela Resort in 2021.

After the inauguration, everyone converged at Grand Central for drinks. It became a big celebration. The UPND government went straight to work, and Gary was appointed Minister in charge of Local Government and Rural Development. I took my mother to witness the swearing-in ceremony of her son, and all the family members who were available in Lusaka made it to State House. There was a breath of fresh air in the country, as people felt they were liberated for the second time. We were excited, and it was party after party at Grand Central.

My entire family with our spouses on my father's 75th birthday.

Left to right (Standing) Stella, Choobe, Alvin, Margaret, Gary, Katendi, Mutinta, Sande, Cholwe, Nchimunya, and Nachilala.

Left to right (seated) Pitcairn Benny, Daddy, my step mother and Munachande

Chapter 20
Island Bliss-Finally Bahamas

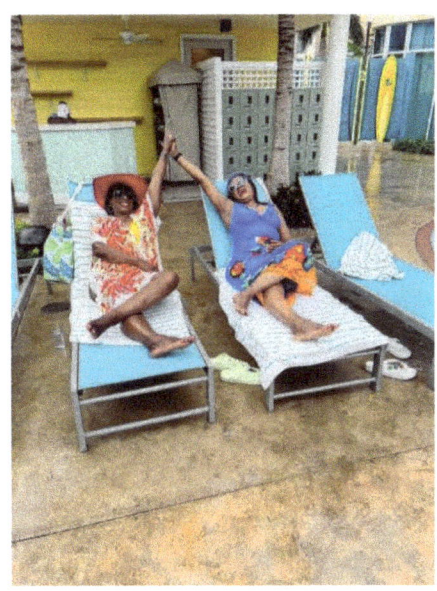

Mutinta and Barbara at the Margaritaville pool side, Nassau, Bahamas.

I planned to take my annual trip to America for re-stocking purposes in October 2023. I took the trip with my friend Barbara Coker. I met Barbara during my stint at Zambia Airways. She struck me as a smart and progressive human being just by the way she did things. She is a few years older than me, and in my mind, I found myself a mentor.

Our itinerary read Lusaka, Dubai, New York, and back the same way exactly one month later. We had plans to visit her daughter Funmi in Washington after doing our business.

We jetted into Dubai and checked into the Radisson Hotel on the Creek. Our mission was to sell our outdated gold chains at the Gold Souk. We rounded the shops around the Souk in search of a good deal for almost three days. Along the way, we decided to do the Desert safari tour. The first time I did the tour, I was with Mwaji and Mashuta, and my eyes were closed throughout the tour because I was frightened. This time, I decided to go with my eyes wide open. Our group tour comprised other nationals from India and South Africa. It was fun, and we connected immediately. Surprisingly, I managed to do the whole desert tour with my eyes open.

We left for New York three days later, and flew for fourteen hours on board a fully booked Emirates flight. New York was buzzing as usual, but had pleasantly cool weather. We found our way to our hotel, the Hilton on 35th Street. Barbara had arranged for her daughter Funmi Coker to join us the same evening we arrived. Funmi came through, and we caught up. She organized dinner for us, and left to go back to her friend in the Bronx.

The next day, we started doing our business. Funmi caught up with us somewhere in the wholesalers. We finished off and headed back to the hotel. We bought our takeaway dinner, and some Tanqueray to accompany us in the evening.

While having a catch-up, Barbara intimated to Funmi that our plan was to visit her in Washington, and end up in Los Angeles, California. We were planning to have a feel of the Walk of Fame. The night went by, and drinks were flowing. Before we realized it, the three of us had downed the Tanqueray. Funmi thought that Los Angeles would be boring, so she started dropping other possible holiday ideas.

By the end of this drink-up, the three of us decided to take a holiday to the Bahamas and Miami instead. We said our goodbyes to Funmi, who was going back to the Bronx. The next day, she called Barbara to ask if we were serious about the Bahamas-Miami holiday, or if it was a Tanqueray-inspired pep talk. We told her to go ahead and book the holiday packages. For me, this was super exciting because I was going to fulfil my dream of going to the Bahamas, after having abandoned the trip thirty-three years earlier.

*Mutinta and Barbara outside the
Lennox Hotel, Miami.*

Funmi started looking for flights and hotels. She did it very easily, and the rest was up to us to pay. We were excited, so we immediately started gearing up for the holiday. We took time off our business schedule, and took a drive to the premier outlets, at the Wood Bury Common with Funmi's friend. He dropped us right in front of a shop called Tommy Bahamas. We entered, shopped around, and mutually agreed that the prices were on the high side. As we continued shopping, the sales girl got us. She used her sales skills to sell the Tommy Bahamas brand and feel, making the price less prominent. We were sold. We were feeling like teenagers, trying outfit after outfit.

The countdown to the Bahamas started. We made sure we acquired a wardrobe of straw hats, sunglasses, earrings, headbands, and beach wear. We were not limited by anything. We set out on a trip to the Bahamas with a plan to spend four nights.

We boarded our Jet Blue flight from John F Kennedy in New York, and flew for three hours to Nassau in the Bahamas. We received a Bahamian welcome characterized by song and dance moves from a local cultural group.

At the immigration counter, the friendly officer asked us what we were going to do in the Bahamas. Barbara narrated the story of how Gary and I abandoned the trip thirty-three years earlier, and how we came to actualize it. He told us to ensure we touched the Fish Fry. "No one comes to the Bahamas without touching the Fish Fry," he advised. He also told us to try their famous cocktail, the Sky Juice.

Funmi set us up at the fresh and enchanting Margaritaville Hotel Resort. The view from our hotel room was characterized by huge cruise ships docking and departing. We made it our home for those four nights.

After checking in, we took a bit of rest, and set out to go to the Fish Fry, which had several restaurants. We walked around with a plan to see which one had our taste. The Taxi driver highly recommended the Twin Brothers restaurant, but we wanted to make our own assessment. We ended up at a restaurant next to Twin Brothers, called "The Big Yard", which we thought housed a lot of the locals.

We sat there with the hope of connecting to one or two locals, and we did. We spoke to a lady and asked her what was a must to see in the Bahamas. She quickly referred us to a taxi driver called Trevor, who seemed to know it all. Trevor assured us that he would do the local city tour with us the next day, and then he quickly got us a gentleman called James for the water tours.

We then ordered the famous Sky juice which the immigration officer highly recommended. Sky juice is a sweet and refreshing Bahamian treat made with Coconut water, sweetened condensed milk and a splash of pineapple juice. It surely did put some smiles on our faces. The locals also taught us how to eat Conch fritters, which we enjoyed very much. The Conch is not only a culinary delight, but also an important part of the Bahamian heritage and identity.

The next day, Trevor picked us up from the hotel and drove us around Nassau. He explained the geography of the island and took us to see the suburbs, the compounds, as well as the Bahamian parliament. He also took us to the famous bat cave and demonstrated how to go in, but we were not brave enough to face the bats. We only managed to take photos on the beautiful stone chair outside the caves.

In the evening, we went back to the Fish Fry, and checked in at the Goldies Karaoke restaurant. We had a seafood meal, danced to their local music, and had our turn at karaoke. We were given a chance to introduce the Bahamians to our local Zambian music, which they embraced with some dance moves. We earned ourselves names in the Bahamas. They called us African sisters or Boss Ladies. The Bahamians loved us, and we loved them too.

The gentleman for the water tours, James, was equally upbeat. He took us through the available tours, and we settled for the package with a beach tour, feeding and swimming with the pigs, jet skiing, banana boat tour, and snorkelling. The next day, he picked us up from the hotel and delivered us to the Nassau Cruise terminal for us to take our day tour.

We cruised around the turquoise water for about 25 minutes, before we reached the beach. We got introduced to the pigs who were responding to human commands. We learnt how to feed them and were warned of how much they love French fries.

One of the ladies we took the tour with lost her bag to the pigs because it contained chips. We also took turns on jet skis and the banana boat. The time for snorkelling came, I knew I did not have the courage and expertise to snorkel, so I passed.

In the evening, Trevor picked us up and dropped us at the famous Atlantis Hotel and Resort. We did some shopping and went through the Aquariums to see different species of fish. On the last day, we took it easy as we needed to re-charge for Miami.

We however managed to go to the Sharkeez restaurant for a meal and watched cruise ships come and go. The next day, we took off for Miami via Fort Lauderdale. We chose to stay at the Lennox Hotel. The hotel arranged a pick-up for us from Fort Lauderdale. We stood outside Fort Lauderdale airport, while waiting for the driver with whom Barbara was in touch. Suddenly, a white vehicle rolled in, and parked in front of us. As it came to a stop, the back doors and the trunk simultaneously opened with an upward swing.

The Tesla X model suddenly looked like a butterfly. It was a spectacular show. While we were admiring the vehicle, the driver got out of the car and shouted, "Barbara." We looked at each other in disbelief. It was our ride after all.

And as the driver was packing our suitcases, our cameras began to work. We took photos of each other, and when the driver realized that we were struggling to take selfies, he came to our rescue.

We arrived at the Lennox Hotel forty-five minutes later, where we were accorded a champagne welcome. Funmi flew in from New York to join us the same evening. She already had our whole tour in Miami mapped out. That evening, we checked in at Espaniola Way, where we had our dinner, and we sang and danced to several birthdays as they were pronounced. The next day, Funmi arranged for us to have Lunch at the former Mansion of Gianni Versace, which is now being run as a five-star hotel. We had a seafood lunch and then walked around the mansion to take photos.

When Lunch was done, we met Gustavo, who took us on a tour of Miami on a go-kart. We did a hope-on-hope-off for Tequila shots at what he said were the places to note in Miami. We stopped over at the Standard Hotel for pictures, and then he drove us to Star Island, where we saw mansions belonging to the world's famous Stars. From there, he took us to the Mandrion, where the rich people in Miami go to chill. After that, he drove us through Ocean Drive, which houses a lot of restaurants.

Mutinta Barbara and Fumni, Go-kart city tour of Miami.

The next day, Barbara and I went shopping at the premier outlets at the Dolphin Mall. Barbara had a lot of hits, and I had a lot of misses on account of size. We went back to the hotel where Funmi was waiting for us to go to the I Satr restaurant, on the rooftop, where we had a night view of Miami.

We had some Purple Rain cocktails and enjoyed some fine dining. Gustavo, our tour guide, advised us that we could have a better view of the Star Mansions from the water, so the next day, we checked in at the Mojito Cruise. It proved to be a better view, as Gustavo advised.

Mutinta and Barbara relaxing at the Nikki Beach, Miami.

By that evening, we were too tired to even dress up, but we managed to get ourselves to the Satr Hotel for some sumptuous dinner. The day we all looked forward to came. It was the last day, and we chose to end it by going to Nikki Beach.

We hired our own Cabana and took time to swim in the Atlantic waters. Apart from a sumptuous beach lunch, we had shots of Tanqueray and a Champagne toast to mark the end of our trip. Our assigned waiter, Felix, was amazing. He constantly looked out for our needs, and said his spirit was at peace with us. Although it was heavy on the pocket, Miami was nice and constantly dripping with fun.

We returned to New York the next day, spent a night at our friend Emeldah Chibuye's place. The next day Emeldah took us out for a meal in Manhattan, and then dropped us at the train station for our trip to Washington. Our idea of going to Washington was to take a proper rest at Funmi's home after the holiday.

Mutinta and Barbara at the Margaritaville Resort, Nassau, Bahamas.

Just one phone call changed the plan to rest. I called my cousin Hankie Malawo, whom I had not seen for many years. He said he was literally thirty minutes away from us. He took a drive to come and see us. He took us on a sightseeing drive to Baltimore, where we had lunch at the Tarks Grill restaurant, and drove back in the evening.

The next day, we had an easy morning, and then we decided to go to Lincoln Square. We took photos by the Lincoln statue, then walked to the World War II, Heroes Square, and then onward to the Cenotaph. From the Cenotaph, we walked over to the White House. Finally, we found ourselves at the Capitol Hill. The white house and Capitol Hill presented tranquil gardens and heavy police presence, but we still managed to take photos. It was a fulfilling holiday to get to see in real life the history and geography we learnt in high school.

Hankie mentioned that his birthday was coming up, and that his wife Mutinta was preparing some birthday spoils that weekend. We checked in at his house on Friday evening, where I met his lovely wife, Mutinta, and my other cousin, Malema. I had not seen Hankie and Malema for years. After a snappy catch-up, I suggested that I buy Hankie a drink for his birthday at a place of his choice. They suggested that we go to the MGM Casino.

The birthday spoils started. We caught up some more, had some drinks, and danced the night away.

The next day, Mutinta cooked a sumptuous lunch for us, after which we caught an Uber for our next engagement that same evening. We were invited to a 50th birthday dinner for Barbara's friend Sattey. We checked in at the Urban Roast, wined, dined, and cheered to the birthday girl.

This marked the end of our month-long trip. The next day, we checked in at the Union Station, to take our train back to New York, to wrap up the business before taking our flight back home.

As I write this particular chapter, we are flying from JFK to Lusaka via Dubai. Although the holiday left us exhausted, it was a wonderful trip, probably the best vacation I have ever taken.

Finally, Bahamas!!! Off my bucket list.

Chapter 21
Lessons from my Mother

The school teacher in my mother always reminded her that she had to keep me in constant check. She is typically one who does not fancy the idea of sparing the rod. I had my fair share of that. My mother devoted herself fully to my upbringing, and she used every resource at her disposal, to shape me into the person I am today. Being a parent in today's world is challenging. Our children think they know better than us, and constantly raise their human rights flag. I give my mother a pat on her back, and thank her immensely for who I have become; those who know me well will attest that I am well-rounded.

My father sent me and my siblings to the village literally every holiday, only to pick us up two days before the beginning of the school term. We got to learn all the hard skills, like tilling the land, and cooking in a huge three-legged cast-iron pot, on big logs of firewood. I also got to learn the art of balancing a bucket full of water on my head, hands-free. I grew up with basic necessities at Kombe Drive in Livingstone, and yet those were the happiest days of my life. The lessons I received from my parents and grandparents, remain more valuable than any material wealth I may have accumulated. I am grateful for this kind of learning because it prepared me to be the person I am today.

My mother sent me and my siblings to the market to sell whatever was sellable, and always encouraged us not to return home with any unsold merchandise. It was unachievable most times, but when I look back, I realize that it was a perfect training ground for me to learn perseverance, a quality that has served me well into adulthood.

I was ushered into the mainstream business world after the Zambian airline closed. I suffered a setback, and thought the world had closed on me when my visa to America was denied, but I persevered, and in the process, I discovered Turkey, which typically made me. The Turkish people are very trusting human beings, and most suppliers gave me an interest, and collateral-free credit line, which helped accelerate my growth. Kudos to: Latifa Kulmanova of Giorgio Visconti, Beshir Nurdag of Zamra Boutique, Ismail Deniz of Famozo Shirt Company, and Cenk Boyraz of the Boyraz Group, the Turkish giants whose shoulders I stand on.

The Turkish experience also taught me that language is an important tool, for any business to take place, something I did not attach as a pre-requisite when I first went to Turkey. Going forward, I made sure I picked up the basics of their language, to help me get around and communicate effectively.

The Genuine group has grown into a recognizable brand. We are customer-centric, more than ever. Without any doubt, we are the fashion leader, and we remain the favourite fashion stop for most occasions in Zambia.

In February 2024, prior to the 1st March International Women's Day celebrations, I received an email from the Managing Director for ABSA, Zambia Ltd, Mrs Mizinga Melu, inviting me to a dinner for Absa women in business. It was a busy period for me as I was doing a crash course at the Zambia Institute of Diplomacy and International Studies. (ZIDIS) I did not reply to Mizinga in time, prompting one of her staff members, Banji Lufungulo, to get in touch with me to confirm my attendance. The ZIDIS program was intense, and I was occupied with assignments and assessments.

I was often tired, so I procrastinated about the decision to attend despite confirming with Banji.

Finally, I told myself that I had to attend, because I had confirmed my attendance. I teamed up with Nachilala and Katendi, who were also invited. It was a worthwhile decision I made to attend. It turned out that I was nominated for the ABSA, Business Resilience Award for 2024. The award was presented to me by our republican Vice President, Mrs WK Mutale Nalumango. I give my heartfelt thanks to ABSA, and the Vice President, for this recognition at a time when the business environment has been experiencing a lot of economic challenges. Post COVID-19, sourcing has become very difficult as the supply chain has been severely disrupted.

Reflecting on my time at high school, I met with different kinds of people from different backgrounds. Some were affluent, and others were from humble homes like mine. Somehow, I found myself mixing with the haves. Their stories made me envious. When I look back now, I do not even know why I associated with the affluent, especially that I had a choice to hang out with girls in my social class. I guess it was the desire to be upwardly mobile.

Television was a big deal when we were growing up, and if we missed television one day, we missed the world. Now here I am, living in my own home in the prestigious Woodlands suburb, with television sets everywhere, including the veranda, and very little or no time to watch. In life, you have to be okay with what you have, and remember that more does not always make you happier.

I was fired twice in my short working life, firstly from Fairmount Hotel, by a person I looked up to as a role model. Alas! I had no idea that she loathed me to a point of having me fired. Then, history repeated itself at Zambia Airways when I was retrenched, while selling the airline. This was obviously done by a hater, who overlooked that critical element. Then, the story about me being married in Turkey also came to light.

Mutinta, receiving the ABSA business resilience award from the Zambian Vice President Mrs WK Mutale Nalumango.

Someone had a desire to dent my image. I suffered slander and ridicule, and my image was dented further by those who knew the truth, but chose to believe and circulate a fake story.

My mother taught me to always be strong, and society left me with no option but to be just that. She added that what does not kill you only makes you stronger. I feel like I have been fighting fires all my life. I had to just wear a layer of thick skin. I have learned to be confident in my own skin, and have become okay with people not liking me; I have no control over that.

I put away the idea of going to university when I opted to join the airline. The normal prescription to life for any growing-up girl, is school, work, marriage, and children. I did not follow this prescribed route. I started with work. The airline job had a lot of travel and allowances, which were very attractive, and it remained attractive for the whole time I was there. The trading part was also lucrative. For some time, the airline experience seemed like a world without end. I was counting what I thought was real money. How could I even think about going to school to be slowed down by the books? And when it was all over, the reality hit home. I was thrown into the real world, to engage with people from different walks of life, and oftentimes, I felt inadequate.

My mother's clarion call for me to go back to school was supported by this inadequacy. Humiliating as it was, I decided to go back to school, and managed to pass with flying colours. My mother told me that school knew no age, when she enrolled in school at an advanced age. She told me that in life, you have to accept where you are, while setting goals for yourself, to compete only with yourself, while centering your actions on achieving growth.

Apart from the inspiration to go to school, she also inspired me to do business, and more importantly, to constantly work. She counselled that the goal should never be to be better than anyone else, but to be better than the way I was yesterday. She also told me that my image is very important, and stressed the importance of dressing to the nines every single day.

My mother told me that she agrees with the notion that a woman's place is in the kitchen, but only to a certain extent, because the whole idea is a relic of the past. She says women are born multitaskers, and she has witnessed many of them breaking barriers, and excelling in every field imaginable. From science and technology, to entrepreneurship and politics, which has had male dominance. The kitchen, which was once seen as a symbol of domesticity, grounding, and limitation has now become a platform for creativity and innovation. Women are now leading the charge of culinary arts, food science and restaurant ownership, shattering the stereotype that cooking is solely a domestic duty. She adds that, with the rise of shared household responsibilities, and gender equality, cooking has become a shared joy, rather than a solitary burden. As women continue to push boundaries, and redefine traditional roles, it is clear that their place is where they ultimately choose to be – be it in the aeroplane, boardroom, laboratory, or indeed the kitchen where they can cook up a storm on their own terms.

My mother also told me that the body is typically like a machine. When one part of a machine breaks down, it can potentially affect other parts, and its efficacy gets compromised. I lived in denial for a long time. When you have insomnia; it is a sign that something is wrong, and it should not be ignored, because the body is meant to shut down at a certain time and recharge for the next day. I had insomnia for a long time.

Insomnia brought about other health-related issues. I traversed between Zambia and South Africa, all in search of wellness for a long time, without stopping to think about the root cause. When it was brought to my attention that I had a kidney problem, I felt like the weight of the world had crushed me.

It was in 2008, and we are now in 2024. I have been loyal to instructions from Gracia. She counselled me that I went to see her at the right time. According to the National Kidney Foundation, 10% of the population worldwide is affected by chronic kidney disease. Most of them do not know it because they have neglected to check.

It's important to listen to your body, and it's more important to always have routine medical check-ups. It is also important to identify the stressors in your life, and be bold enough to address them. Masking takes away your freedom, and consequently, your quality of life. Being able to speak out is not a weakness, but a strength, because transparency gives you the freedom, and wisdom to touch others through your story.

I regretted judging my mother so harshly when she left my father. She laboured to explain that she could no longer be with him. She prayed that I would understand her decision someday. It did not take long for me to realize and understand that, divorce is actually a solution to a problem. I was 23 years young and naïve, when I got married, and neglected to ask all the pertinent questions, which I should have asked before joining a blended family. After twenty-eight years, and despite so many counselling interventions, our paths still failed to align. I threw in the towel.

*My grandchildren
Matthew-Teo and Kyeya-Mae.*

My story typically mirrors that of my mother. Neither my devotion to my husband, nor the hard work I put in for my family, could prevent my marriage from failing the test of, "To the exclusion of all others." In my case, I had been married for twenty-eight years. I just could not see how I could accommodate an extra budget for formula and nursery school rhymes in my golden years. Just like in my mother's case, I had no power to change anything. This discovery broke my heart, and worsened our existing estrangement.

It took prominence, and watered down all the other challenges I thought we had. It also put to bed all hopes of a reconciliation. I finally picked up some courage to break the news to my mother. She looked down upon hearing the news, and I noticed that she was constantly holding back tears. She wondered whether it was a generational curse. I was also about to burst into tears, but managed to hold back, and assured her that contrary to her thoughts, we are a lineage of strong and actualized women. Through spiritual counselling, I learned to forgive, even where no apology was rendered, because forgiveness is another self-love strategy.

My mother also told me to be resilient, because life is not always a straight line; some days are good, and others are bad. She told me that for every bitter lemon cast at me, I should make a lemonade.

My trials taught me patience, and to be able to control my emotions, in order to make the right decisions. My life-changing decision was to walk away from a life I had known for decades.

I walked out of my marriage not because I was happy to, but because I was left with no choice. No one gets married only to divorce, but it is inevitable to walk away from someone you love, for your own sanity. I had to learn to be strong in my own identity.

It's called self-love, and more importantly, it is self-preservation. Self-love is not vanity but sanity. You cannot control another person's thinking and actions, but you certainly can control how you respond to them. It is very easy to commit to a relationship, but it takes a lot of work to remain there. Staying on was hard, and walking away was even harder. It is synonymous with open heart surgery, without any anaesthetic intervention.

It is a difficult process to heal from someone who promised to love you forever. Apart from the inner struggles, you are judged harshly by people, who seem to know your inside story better than you, and turn a blind eye to your emotional state. That is the nature of man.

I invite everyone who is reading this memoir of my trials and triumphs, to always remember that there are always two sides to a story: there are positive and negative perceptions out there, but society's nature is to thrive on negative ones.

Finally, I am here saying, that my life has not been perfect. I have done some things right, and made a few wrong turns, but there was a lot of learning in the process.

Now, here is the cherry on my iced cake, which waters down all the negatives. God gave me the most beautiful children: my adorable daughter, Mwaji Mbalazi, and my son, Majestic Mashuta Kayumba. Mwaji gave me a gorgeous son-in-law, Musonda Mbalazi. Through the two, I am now enjoying the style and title of Grandmother.

I thank God for making me live to see these two munchkins. Mathew-Teo and Kyeya-Mae. The two bring out my inner child; we fight and play like we are age mates. Somehow, they know that they can take advantage of Grandma, and their bedtime is extended when they sleep over at mine.

I have started growing my knowledge of dinosaurs, because that is quite a dominant topic from Teo. Our aim is to own several different species one day. As for Kyeya, my dresser is her favourite spot. She often tries out my makeup, and eventually makes a mess of it. We are also getting to understand each other, as her speech is quickly beginning to form; she parrots everything Teo says. It is indeed a different kind of love.

Epilogue

Four generations: Beatrice, Mutinta, Mwaji, and Kyeya.

Writing this book has provided me with a platform to share my life story authentically, just as I have experienced it. Having lived every moment, twenty-four- seven, up to my current age, I believe no one can narrate my story better than myself. The opportunity to tell my story has granted me a unique sense of freedom, and transparency, serving as the most therapeutic endeavour I could give myself.

I talk to myself many a time. My inner voice speaks to numerous issues. It constantly reminds me of my life goals, successes, and failures. It sounds like a typical daily checklist.

I chose to call my book "Inspired", because I was greatly inspired by my mother, and it is my earnest prayer that this book will inspire someone too.

When you are inspired by someone, you try to follow their path. My mother inspired me to embrace the process of continuous growth, without forgetting that as long as I continue to live, I should strive for more growth. The growth process is, however, synonymous with a pendulum. Sometimes, you feel accomplished, yet oftentimes, the feeling of inadequacy creeps in. In life, you can have so much, and yet concentrate on what you lack, forgetting to be grateful for what you already have.

Apart from my mother's counsel, I also learned a few lessons from the school of life. The decisions I made in life have given me a springboard to navigate my life in an upwardly mobile trajectory. As a young girl, I read a book titled Rich Dad, Poor Dad, by Robert Kiyosaki, which became my life manual. I learned that mindset is everything: to believe in myself and associate with people who are smarter than me; to take business risks, to make the right investments, and to manage money effectively.

Kiyosaki preaches that, one must make more money than one spends. I learned the importance of financial literacy, intelligence, and that as you slowdown in life, money must typically work for you. I also learned about assets and liabilities, and what course of action to take when an asset becomes a liability.

When Comfort Lodge became a liability, I put away the sentimental value, and painfully let it go. I am hoping that the decisions I have made in life, will take care of me going forward.

Narrating my story is an upwardly mobile endeavour, and while it may not be flawless, I take pride in having lived it. To those inspired by this narrative, I encourage you to share your stories, in order to inspire others. To those who celebrate me, and those who just tolerate me, but have reached this far in reading my book, thank you. With this black pen in my hand, I proudly declare this as the definitive version of my story.

Time flew by in the whirlwind of fashion, but all my dreams became a reality. I was inspired to become an air hostess, to get married and have children, to go back to university, to become a successful entrepreneur, and above all, to be a woman of God. I savoured every moment. All things considered, I have lived life to the fullest.

I am grateful to the Divine, for the protection and guidance throughout my life, as well as the wisdom, patience, and courage to write. I have broken free from the shackles of my past, but have taken ownership of my story, as it cannot be changed. I have embraced my triumphs and refuse to be defined by the setbacks. Through my mistakes, I have gained invaluable wisdom, and I remain receptive to new lessons, which the universe may bestow upon me.

There is a new inspiration brewing inside of me. Now, it's time to hang my fashion boots, and pass the torch to my daughter Mwaji, in order to leave a lasting legacy.

As my car pulls into my driveway, I bid farewell to my loved ones, as I embark on a new chapter in my life, in a distant land. "Act Two" awaits, filled with endless possibilities.

Hasta luego, amigas!

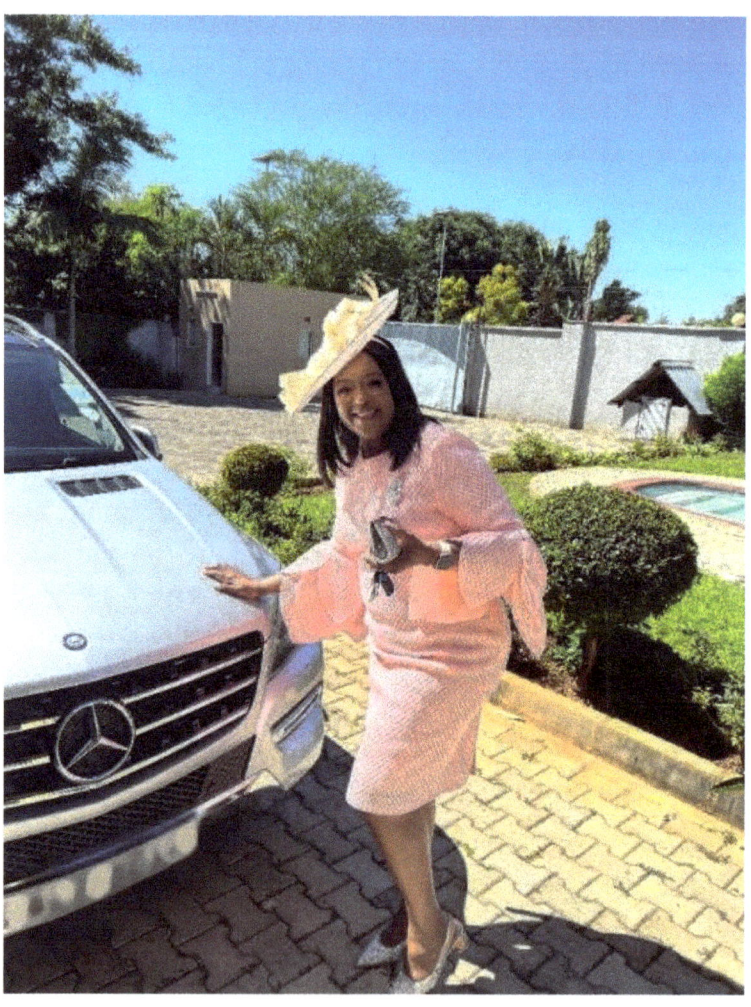